CONGRESSIONAL
ETHICS

CONGRESSIONAL ETHICS

☆ ☆ ☆ ☆ ☆ ☆ ☆ ☆ ☆ ☆ ☆ ☆ ☆ ☆ ☆ ☆ ☆ ☆

The View from the House

EDMUND BEARD

and STEPHEN HORN

THE BROOKINGS INSTITUTION
Washington, D.C.

THE BROOKINGS INSTITUTION is an independent organization devoted to nonpartisan research, education, and publication in economics, government, foreign policy, and the social sciences generally. Its principal purposes are to aid in the development of sound public policies and to promote public understanding of issues of national importance.

The Institution was founded on December 8, 1927, to merge the activities of the Institute for Government Research, founded in 1916, the Institute of Economics, founded in 1922, and the Robert Brookings Graduate School of Economics and Government, founded in 1924.

The Board of Trustees is responsible for the general administration of the Institution, while the immediate direction of the policies, program, and staff is vested in the President, assisted by an advisory committee of the officers and staff. The by-laws of the Institution state: "It is the function of the Trustees to make possible the conduct of scientific research, and publication, under the most favorable conditions, and to safeguard the independence of the research staff in the pursuit of their studies and in the publication of the results of such studies. It is not a part of their function to determine, control, or influence the conduct of particular investigations or the conclusions reached."

The President bears final responsibility for the decision to publish a manuscript as a Brookings book. In reaching his judgment on the competence, accuracy, and objectivity of each study, the President is advised by the director of the appropriate research program and weighs the views of a panel of expert outside readers who report to him in confidence on the quality of the work. Publication of a work signifies that it is deemed a competent treatment worthy of public consideration but does not imply endorsement of conclusions or recommendations.

The Institution maintains its position of neutrality on issues of public policy in order to safeguard the intellectual freedom of the staff. Hence interpretations or conclusions in Brookings publications should be understood to be solely those of the authors and should not be attributed to the Institution, to its trustees, officers, or other staff members, or to the organizations that support its research.

Foreword

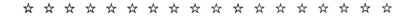

ALWAYS a matter of importance, the ethical behavior of public officials occasionally becomes a matter of particular concern. A few years before Watergate, when the improprieties of certain legislators reached the headlines and eventually the courts, both the Senate and the House of Representatives hastened to establish "ethics" committees. After Watergate, the Senate and House passed bills controlling campaign fund-raising and spending. But between such periods of heightened concern about unethical practices, there are long quiet stretches. This work is a report on how members of the House perceived the ethical issue during the relatively quiet time immediately before the Nixon-Agnew administration. At another relatively quiet time—after the preoccupation with Watergate has receded—it will be appropriate to renew the inquiry to learn whether one Congress by and large is like another or whether Watergate has effected a change in legislators' perceptions of ethics.

Like an earlier Brookings study by Charles L. Clapp, *The Congressman: His Work as He Sees It* (1963), this essay focuses on the perspective from within Congress. It demonstrates that members of the House consider many of the criticisms leveled at Congress to be unjustified or unreasonable. Representatives of both parties cite constraints and dilemmas that they feel are unappreciated by critics among their constituents and members of the press. The authors highlight these dilemmas in discussing the congressmen's attitudes and practices with respect to campaign finance, staff use, office funding, and outside financial investment and business involvement, and analyze the extent of controls imposed by the House itself on ethical transgressions. They conclude by evaluating the merits of various suggested reforms of congressional behavior and considering the likelihood of their adoption.

Edmund Beard, assistant professor of politics at the University of Massachusetts, was recently a research associate in the Brookings Governmental Studies program. Stephen Horn, president of California State College at Long Beach, has in the past been a legislative aide to former Senator Thomas Kuchel of California as well as a senior fellow at Brookings. Horn designed the questionnaire and conducted most of the interviews; Beard was primarily responsible for the analysis of the results. Both concur in the presentation and findings.

The authors wish to express their thanks to Gilbert Y. Steiner and Leonard Goodwin for constant encouragement and assistance. Various drafts of the study were criticized by Stanley Bach, Jeffrey Berry, Stephen Hess, Richard P. Nathan, Judith H. Parris, Steven Schack, James L. Sundquist, and several anonymous readers. Radmila Reinhart typed the manuscript, and Tadd Fisher edited it. The help of all these people is acknowledged and appreciated.

KERMIT GORDON
President

July 1975
Washington, D.C.

Contents

☆ ☆ ☆ ☆ ☆ ☆ ☆ ☆ ☆ ☆ ☆ ☆ ☆ ☆ ☆ ☆ ☆ ☆

Text Tables

Appendix Table

ONE Introduction

INDIVIDUAL MEMBERS of Congress are constantly faced with real or potential ethical dilemmas as they hire staff, frank mail, raise campaign funds, and cast or withhold a particular vote. Precious few guidelines exist to help. In the hard cases a member is compelled to make a decision according to a personal standard of right and wrong and to hope that he or she will be judged neither fool nor scoundrel.

What are these personal standards? Aside from a few memoirs—some of them self-serving—and fragmentary interview data reported in the press during a cause célèbre, congressmen's perceptions of legislative propriety have been largely unknown. This fact motivated the inquiry that we report on here. Although our data, derived from a cross-section of a Congress that expired the year Richard Nixon first became President, are admittedly imperfect, we believe them to be the best that exist and that in the long run the Ninetieth Congress will turn out to be not so very different from most others.

Our particular intent was to learn if there are common standards among members of the House of Representatives. We were concerned, too, with how members view complaints about their behavior, how widespread they perceive unethical conduct to be in the House, and what they think of various proposals for legislating ethical standards.

Just as the Watergate scandals have recently focused much attention on the executive branch, a series of events in the 1960s heightened public concern over congressional behavior. In 1962 Robert G. (Bobby) Baker, secretary to the Democratic

1

majority in the Senate, was accused of bribery, influence peddling, and tax evasion. Baker, a friend and protégé of Lyndon B. Johnson while the latter was Senate majority leader, was closely associated with many Senate leaders. He was charged with having used these connections to further his and his associates' business interests, particularly in obtaining contracts for his vending machine company. After Baker was found to have become a millionaire while serving in his $19,000-a-year job, he was forced to resign. Baker's conviction in 1967 for tax evasion, conspiracy, and theft was in many ways an anticlimax. His shady and often illegal operations had long before cast a cloud of suspicion over the entire Senate leadership.

The Baker scandal was still in the news when two more events shook both the House and the Senate. Congressman Adam Clayton Powell of New York had long been one of the more flamboyant members of the House. As chairman of the Education and Labor Committee, he had also been one of its most effective ones. Possessed of equal measures of wit, charm, and legislative prowess, he was a primary force behind liberal social legislation. By the mid 1960s, however, his reputation had undergone a noticeable transformation. Long and well-publicized vacations at his Bimini Island retreat during congressional sessions and equally well-publicized visits to European nightspots in the company of female staff members while on congressional research trips had sparked public criticism. Then Powell was convicted of libel in his native New York and subsequently of civil and criminal contempt when he refused to pay the damages awarded. For a time Powell visited his district only on Sundays when he could not be arrested on the civil contempt charges. After the criminal finding, he avoided the district altogether.

Other complaints were leveled at Powell for misuse of public funds after it was revealed that his estranged wife was receiving $20,578 a year from his staff payroll while she lived in Puerto Rico. In addition, a House Administration Committee investigation concluded that Powell and members of his committee staff had improperly charged private travel expenses to committee funds, sometimes employing false names to hide the practice.

Public outrage over the total image of Powell's behavior continued to swell. His own committee grew restive over his absenteeism, capricious actions as chairman, and delay of popular legislation. The criticism crossed political and racial lines as many black leaders became irritated by his erratic legislative behavior or dismayed by his public indiscretion. Finally, the House acted, excluding Powell from the Eighty-ninth Congress. When the Supreme Court later ruled that Powell must be admitted, he was received into the Ninety-first Congress but was first fined $25,000 and stripped of seniority. As in the Baker case, many House members believed that long-term damage was already done. Powell's actions, and the apparent delay by the House in dealing with them, had engendered or reinforced in many minds an image of congressmen as lazy, irresponsible, or self-serving.

In 1966, while the furor over Powell developed, the Senate encountered problems of its own. Senator Thomas Dodd of Connecticut became the object of a series of published reports alleging personal use of campaign funds, double billing of public and private sources for travel and other expenses, and related misdeeds. Many of the charges were aired in Drew Pearson and Jack Anderson's widely circulated column. Coming soon after the Baker affair and in the midst of the Powell controversy, the revelations had a damaging public impact. This situation was not helped when an initial Senate investigation that cleared Dodd of any wrongdoing was subsequently discredited by continuing Pearson/Anderson revelations. Following a second investigation, the Senate ultimately censured Dodd. Once again, however, the damage was done.

The scandals noted above received wide television coverage. Public approval of congressional performance and public respect for individual members of Congress fell dramatically. Worse, senators and representatives found that wrongdoing by one of their colleagues reflected badly on all of them. In the public mind, the sins of one were not isolated aberrations but the likely tendencies of all.

The Senate and House reacted, if only out of an instinct for self-preservation. In the past, Congress had been extremely reluctant to become involved in setting and enforcing ethical standards for congressmen. A partial explanation may lie in comments Adam Powell made just before his exclusion: "Let he who is without sin cast the first stone. There is no one here who does not have a skeleton in his closet. I know and I know them by name."[1] The Baker, Powell, and Dodd affairs, however, created public pressure that could not be ignored. New "ethics" committees were formed (the Select Committee on Standards and Conduct in the Senate and the Committee on Standards of Official Conduct in the House) and charged with a watchdog function. Whether those committees were expected to set standards and actively investigate apparent shortcomings or to achieve the public relations purpose of reassuring and tempering public opinion is one of the interests of this study. Certain other changes were subsequently legislated, particularly with respect to campaign financing. The nature of these new regulations—what is included, what is not, and why—is another interest.

The 1960s undoubtedly made congressmen more aware of the importance of ethical questions and more aware too of the low public image of congressional behavior. This study was designed to analyze that new awareness as well as to investigate how accurate or relevant the public concern is. The public seems to demand a certain level of "purity" from its elected representatives. We will discuss not only whether the public gets the purity it demands but also whether congressmen think such demands are justified, realistic, or even feasible.

If legislators' perceptions of congressional behavior do not differ sharply from those of groups outside Congress, there is

1. *Congressional Quarterly Almanac* (1967), p. 538.

no issue. If the perceptions do differ, however, external groups must find some way of reforming legislators, or legislators must attend to educating their constituents to the complexity of ethical problems. The least healthy situation in a democracy is one in which legislators and constituents not only have different perceptions of what constitutes ethical legislative behavior but also are unaware of their differences.

☆　☆　☆　☆　☆　☆　☆　☆　☆　☆　☆　☆　☆　☆　☆　☆　☆　☆

THE DATA for this study, which was conducted during the Ninetieth Congress, were obtained in two ways. First, we distributed a lengthy questionnaire, consisting of descriptions of forty-four hypothetical situations that might constitute problems or dilemmas, to a random sample of 50 of the 435 members of the House of Representatives. Of these, forty-three returned the questionnaire. We asked the respondents to rate each hypothetical situation according to their ethical judgment of the behavior described and to give their opinion as to the prevalence of the behavior. Thus the responses permitted us in turn to rate congressional perceptions of the hypothetical situations. Next, we conducted structured, open-ended interviews with the entire random sample of fifty congressmen. These interviews took place in the members' offices and lasted from a half hour to nearly two hours, the majority taking about an hour. The respondents were guaranteed anonymity.

By combining the data from the questionnaire and from the interviews, we hoped to gain a comprehensive view of congressional ethics. In answering a questionnaire, the respondent replies to questions that the researcher has chosen as important but that may not touch on what the respondent considers to be central to the issue. In a structured, open-ended interview, on the other hand, the respondent has an opportunity to move beyond the limitations of the question and to shed light on what he, rather than the researcher, thinks is significant.

One problem with a study of this kind, however, is that attitudes do not provide a sure guide to behavior. But in this case, they do provide an idea of what congressmen perceive to be the "best" behavior that can be expected of them by both their peers and their constituents. Congressmen may not conform in their actions to the verbal standards they set for themselves, but at least they are unlikely to be *more ethical* than their codes. Congressmen's perceptions of the behavior of their colleagues, if expressed honestly, are the next best thing to direct knowledge of congressional behavior.

To obtain additional perceptions of congressional behavior, we also distributed the questionnaire to randomly chosen samples of the congressional press corps, Washington-based lobbyists, congressional staff, and legislative liaison personnel of the executive branch. These findings appear in the appendix.

The forty-three congressional respondents to the questionnaire did not precisely reflect the makeup of the House of Representatives of the Ninetieth Congress, second session, from which the sample was drawn. At that time 57 percent of the members of the House were Democrats and 43 percent were Republicans. The respondents, on the other hand, included nineteen Democrats (44 percent) and twenty-four Republicans (56 percent); so the relative party strengths in the House were almost exactly reversed in the sample. In addition to slighting the Democratic party, the sample specifically underrepresents southern Democrats, an important group. Several southern Democrats among the original random selection declined to return the questionnaire. Since these members were interviewed at length, however, the weakness of underrepresentation on the questionnaire was partially overcome.

On the other hand, the questionnaire sample overrepresents the western states, western Republicans in particular. Very close correlations were attained for the northeastern and north central states. A comparison of the geographical distribution and party affiliations of the sample and of the House of Representatives is presented in table 2-1.

Table 2-1. *Comparison of Geographical Distribution and Party Affiliations of Questionnaire Sample and of the House of Representatives, Ninetieth Congress*
Percent

Region	Proportion of total		Proportion of Democrats		Proportion of Republicans	
	Sample	House of Representatives	Sample	House of Representatives	Sample	House of Representatives
Northeast	26	25	14	15	12	10
North Central	30	29	7	11	23	18
West	28	16	12	9	16	7
South	16	30	11	22	5	8
Total	100	100	44	57	56	43

"Junior" members—those serving less than four terms—also were overrepresented in the sample. Sixty-three percent of the sample were junior members and 37 percent had served more than four terms; the comparable proportions in the House during the Ninetieth Congress were 48 percent and 52 percent respectively. Since power in the House is closely associated with seniority, such biases in the sample must be noted. The differences were not large, however, and were alleviated by interviewing senior members who declined to answer the questionnaire.

We asked respondents to rate the conduct described in the hypothetical situations as clearly unethical (scored 1), probably unethical (scored 2), probably ethical (scored 3), or clearly ethical (scored 4). Then we asked whether most (scored 1), many (scored 2), few (scored 3), or none (scored 4) of the members of the House of Representatives would engage in such conduct if the opportunity arose. We subjected the ratings given these questions by the 43 congressional and 357 noncongressional respondents to a factor analysis in order to determine whether the questions would cluster into groups, as expected.[1] The factor analysis showed eight groups of questions for the "ethical judgment" measure and eight for the "prevalence" measure (see table 2-2). A respondent's score on each group is the average of his scores on the included questions. These scores are more reliable than scores on individual items.

1. A principal components solution with varimaxorthogonal rotations. The squared multiple regression coefficients were entered in the diagonals of the correlation matrix, and the number of rotations corresponded to the number of eigenvalues of 1 or greater. Items that loaded at least 0.30 on a factor and much lower on other factors were regarded as candidates for a group. The intercorrelations among questions were examined and only those that added to the reliability of a group were chosen. A similar procedure was used in forming groups from the separate questions asking how widely practiced each hypothetical activity might be; i.e., a separate factor analysis was carried out on those responses. There was a strong tendency for the same questions to cluster separately in both analyses. A final decision was made on which questions to include in the groups on the basis of their appearance in the "ethical judgment" and the "frequency" factors.

Table 2-2. *Congressional Respondents' Scores on the Questionnaire, by Item Group*

	Mean score	
Group and subject	Judgment of practice[a]	Extent of practice[b]
1. Use of staff for partisan purposes	1.55 (0.60)	2.62 (0.56)
2. Personal use of campaign funds	1.84 (0.53)	2.86 (0.50)
3. Favors from private interests	1.88 (0.55)	2.58 (0.56)
4. Nepotism	2.29 (0.97)	2.88 (0.52)
5. Insertions in *Congressional Record* favoring campaign contributors	2.38 (0.79)	2.33 (0.78)
6. Promoting personal interests that coincide with constituent interests	2.49 (0.68)	2.09 (0.53)
7. Ties with law firms	2.50 (0.67)	2.31 (0.61)
8. Use of campaign funds for constituent service	3.03 (0.75)	2.02 (0.72)

Note: Figures in parentheses denote standard deviation.
a. Scoring for judgment of practice:
　　1 = clearly unethical　　3 = probably ethical
　　2 = probably unethical　4 = clearly ethical
b. Scoring for extent of practice:
　　1 = most congressmen　　3 = few
　　2 = many　　　　　　　4 = none

Responses to the Questionnaire

The average scores of the congressmen responding to the questionnaire produced the rank order of groups of questions shown in table 2-2, progressing from that considered least ethical to that considered most ethical.

The individual items in each of these groups of questions will be analyzed in later chapters in conjunction with the interview data. Certain interesting patterns do emerge, however, from the groups themselves. The order from fewest to most thought likely to engage in a given activity is nepotism (group 4), personal use of campaign funds (group 2), use of staff for partisan electoral purposes (group 1), accepting favors from private interests (group 3), *Congressional Record* insertions favoring campaign contributors (group 5), ties with law firms (group 7), promoting personal financial interests that coincide with constituent interests (group 6), and using campaign funds for constituent service (group 8). With the exception of group 4, dealing with nepotism, the rankings are complementary— those activities considered least ethical were also judged least likely to be practiced. There are important differences of degree, however, as we will point out later. The rating of nepotism as least likely to occur undoubtedly reflects the fact that the employment of relatives by any public official, including congressmen, was made illegal in 1967.[2]

The employment of relatives has always been an easy issue for a challenger to exploit, and for that reason many members had refrained from the practice before the legislation outlawing it, although others clearly had not. Despite the law, members of Congress do not see nepotism as particularly unethical.[3] Perhaps they agree with the comment of Mayor Richard Daley of Chicago that nepotism is the hiring of *incompetent* relatives. Many of the respondents reported that they saw nothing wrong with hiring a wife, husband, or brother since their relatives were apt to be knowledgeable about the district's (and the congressman's) needs as well as loyal and hardworking. They acknowledged, however, the ease with which the practice can be made to appear improper to the public eye.

The ordering of the groups is revealing, since it seems to

2. Section 221 of the Postal Revenue and Federal Salary Act of 1967. Section 221 also covers the President and would have prohibited, for example, President Kennedy's appointment of Robert Kennedy as attorney general. A grandfather clause allowing the continued employment of relatives hired before the effective date of the legislation was included.

3. Members expressed resentment at the statute but explained that it had passed because after the Adam Powell affair congressmen were afraid to vote against anything that had an "ethics" angle.

progress from behavior that redounds to the congressman's personal benefit, through behavior benefiting both the congressman and certain constituent groups, to activity that benefits the district as a whole. Activity in which a member receives cash or items of value is deemed far more unethical than business investments or the promotion of specialized interests. Finally, the use of campaign funds to serve constituents is considered quite proper.

Congressional response varied greatly on each group of questions, indicating disagreement about the propriety of the activities. Some congressmen defended and others denounced each of the types of activity hypothesized. The congressmen also disagreed on the extent of such conduct in Congress. Some described the behavior as rampant within the House, and others said just the opposite. The lack of any common standards of proper behavior was evident. The differences may simply demonstrate that the House of Representatives has its normal share of both cynics and innocents or, what may be more likely, that the average congressman does not have a very clear idea of what his colleagues are doing—particularly in their less public affairs. The findings are useful, nonetheless, because they indicate that many congressmen believe that certain activities commonly considered to be of uncertain propriety are quite legitimate, and many (not always the same individuals) do not see much wrongdoing by their colleagues. Together, these tendencies have the effect of slowing further regulation or reform.

The Effect of Variables on Response

We conducted several tests to determine if certain variables seemed to determine response—for example, if Republicans appeared to maintain more stringent standards of behavior or if senior members had views different from those of their juniors. The following variables were examined:

1. Party.
2. Seniority (members with more than four terms in the

House were considered "senior"; those with one to four terms, "junior").

3. Geographical location of the district (four broad categories—Northeast, North Central, West, and South—were used).

4. Urban-rural characteristics of districts.

5. Previous occupation (those in law compared with those in business).

6. Committee status (chairmen, subcommittee chairmen, or ranking minority members compared with the others).

7. Service on "interest," or "pork," committees (for example, agriculture, banking and currency, commerce, interior, merchant marine, veterans, post office, public works) compared with service on "duty" committees (such as armed services, foreign affairs, science and astronautics, atomic energy, judiciary, District of Columbia, government operations).[4]

8. Childhood community (those of over 100,000 population compared with those below 25,000).

9. Age (members under fifty compared with those over fifty).

10. Political conservatism versus political liberalism (judgment was made by inspecting the conservative coalition ratings of Americans for Constitutional Action, the Committee on Political Education, and *Congressional Quarterly*).

A "t" test was used to determine the significance of the differences between the groups. Results falling within the 0.05 level of probability (employing a two-tailed test) were deemed significant.

The findings were striking in their inconclusiveness. In the ethical judgments of the hypothetical behavior, no significant patterns emerged by party, by seniority, or by location of the

---

4. The distinction is not always easy to make. Pork, or interest, committees are those that offer opportunities for members to distribute rich economic rewards to their districts and constituents. The nature of duty committees, however, somewhat limits such opportunities.

district in any of the groups of questions. Nor were there significant differences between members who had grown up in a small community and those who had come from larger cities, between members who served on interest, or pork, committees and those on duty committees, or between the chairmen and ranking minority members and their colleagues.

The congressmen who had been lawyers before their election to the House believed that promoting a constituent interest that happens to coincide with a personal financial interest (group 6) was more ethical than did those members who had previously been engaged in banking or business. The difference in the responses was significant and may reflect the lawyers' attempt to justify continued law practice, even though a congressman's personal financial interest in a law practice can present potentially troublesome conflicts. This is particularly the case when private interests seek out a congressman's firm precisely because of his position. Thus the lawyers may feel a greater need to legitimize their practices. In later sections of this study, however, we will make it clear that many congressmen believe that continued practice of law after election to Congress is a particularly improper involvement because of the opportunities for abuse.

While former lawyers, businessmen, and bankers differed only slightly in their ethical judgment of maintaining ties with law firms (group 7), congressmen under fifty and those over fifty did show a significant difference in their judgment of the practice. The younger members found the practice to be more ethical (mean score = 2.73) than did the older ones (mean score = 2.21). This finding could be easily explained if the younger members generally were also those with less seniority in the House. In that case they might have found the practice more legitimate because they were less secure in the House and faced greater risks in giving up outside affiliations. There is not, however, a perfect match between the chronologically younger members and those with less seniority. Furthermore, for group 7, we found no difference in response on the basis of seniority; among both senior and junior congressmen there was an almost identical distribution of those who regarded the practice as ethical and those who thought it unethical. The difference on group 7 between younger and older members is thus difficult to explain.

The second half of the questionnaire, which asked how prevalent the specified activity would be among congressmen if the opportunity arose, produced an equally wide range of response. Once again, however, it was difficult to discern any underlying patterns that might explain the differences. The same ten variables were applied to these responses with few meaningful results.

The size of a respondent's hometown and the character of his district were related to differences in the extent to which campaign funds were thought to be used for constituency service (group 8) and the extent to which staff was used for partisan purposes (group 1). Those members of Congress serving from highly urban districts judged that significantly more of their colleagues engage in group 8 activities than did members raised in or serving rural areas. Members from highly urban districts also considered group 1 behavior to be more ethical and more widely practiced than did the more rural representatives. These responses presumably reflect the varying needs and expectations of different constituencies.

Those members serving on interest, or pork, committees believed that significantly more congressmen engage in group 3 activity (the acceptance of favors from private interests) than did the members of duty committees. Private groups are more likely to be involved with the work of pork committees than with duty committees. The fact that members of the former committees saw more acceptance of special favors indicates that the practice is more widespread in precisely those committees where one might expect it. Members on duty committees are less often approached with favors. Any assumption on their part that the remainder of the House is treated similarly is unwarranted.

Although the attempt to make sense out of the wide variety of congressional responses by delineating subgroups that fell consistently to one extreme or the other on any of the questions proved generally unsuccessful, one finding did stand out beyond that of the disparity itself. Congressmen perceive that their colleagues engage more widely in the various types of behavior described than would be expected from the respondents' judgment of the propriety of the acts. Groups 1, 2, and 3 were all rated somewhere between "probably unethical" and "clearly unethical." When asked how many of their colleagues would participate in such activity if given the opportunity, however, the respondents as a whole felt that somewhere between "many" and "few" would, with groups 1 and 3 rated quite near the midpoint. Group 1 (use of staff for partisan purposes) exemplifies the problem. Only three respondents ranked this item in the "probably ethical" or "clearly ethical" half of the range, but thirteen believed that most or many of their colleagues use their staffs for partisan purposes.

Only two groups of questions held to the pattern that what is considered unethical can also be presumed to be not widely practiced. Group 8 (use of campaign funds for constituent service) was rated 3.03 (3 = probably ethical) and 2.02 (2 = many) and group 4 (nepotism) was rated 2.29 (2 = probably unethical) and 2.88 (3 = few). Group 6 (promoting personal interest) fell directly at the midpoint on the "probably ethical"/"probably unethical" range but was judged likely to be practiced by many. Group 5 (insertions in *Congressional Record*) was rated closer to "probably unethical" and yet was considered more likely to attract many congressmen than few. This interesting finding indicates that behavior that is considered to be improper even by congressmen themselves is nevertheless widely practiced in the House. The apparent gap between standards and performance will be discussed at length in later sections.

THREE Conflict of Interest

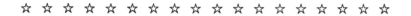

ANY CONGRESSIONAL behavior that is not designed to advance the common interests of constituents and country might be termed conflict of interest. But this generalization is not useful, neglecting as it does the many complexities and ambiguities of congressional service. At one extreme, conflict of interest becomes corruption; at the other, it merges with the legitimate representation of constituents.

A congressman is approached by many people other than the residents of his district—his own or the opposing party's leadership, colleagues, the President or his agents, and a host of representatives of private interests seeking the congressman's voice and vote. These groups can create divided loyalties for the congressman, and they can also offer a variety of material and nonmaterial rewards for his cooperation.

Congressmen lament about the special burdens and contradictions that characterize their responsibilities—problems they feel the public and the media do not recognize. A legislator is simultaneously expected to represent the interests of his constituency and of the nation as a whole, but these interests may not always be identical, and, even when they are substantially complementary, other claims to limited federal resources may be more valid. This ambiguity of role creates some of the most intense ethical dilemmas faced by congressmen.

The problem of conflicting national and constituent interests is complicated because most legislators feel that if they consistently oppose the interests of the constituency, even when those interests are quite narrowly conceived, their prospects for continued tenure are bleak, and they are likely to be replaced by more compliant representatives. This situation forces a pattern of ad hoc compromise whereby competing images of constituency interests and national interests are held in tandem while the representative sometimes attempts to "educate" his district and at other times works wholeheartedly for narrow constituent benefits. Some legislators see their role merely as that of a promoter of constituency interests and never confront such conflicts. For a great many legislators, however, such dilemmas are a real part of congressional life.

Related problems arise over the meaning of "constituency." Is a constituency simply a majority of the population or of the voting-age population? Is it the members of one's own party since the other party would have elected someone else and in many cases worked actively in opposition? Is the constituency composed primarily of those who contributed the major part of one's campaign expenses and without whom one might not have been elected? Is the district characterized by its largest employers? These are questions that confront all legislators and that touch in one way or another on many of the unresolved issues discussed in this study.

In 1960 the Association of the Bar of the City of New York published a detailed study of conflict of interest in the executive branch. The definition used was the clash or the appearance of clash between the "interest of the government official (and the public) in the proper administration of his office" and "the official's interest in his private economic affairs."[1] The bar association report emphasized the interrelation of the public and private sectors of American society and devoted much attention to the difficulties of recruiting qualified officials if the standards of "purity" are too stringent. The role of a congressman is considerably different from that of an official in the executive branch, however, and it is well to make the distinction clear.

1. Association of the Bar of the City of New York, *Conflict of Interest and Federal Service* (Harvard University Press, 1960), p. 3.

Five Possible Conflicts

One analyst of the executive branch conflict of interest law passed in 1961 has defined five areas of possible conflict: self-dealing by a public official, discretionary transfer of economic value to a public official from a private source, assistance by public officials to private parties dealing with the government, post-employment assistance by former public officials to private parties dealing with the government, and private gain derived from information acquired in an official capacity.[2] Using this list as a guide, we will illustrate the distinction claimed above between the executive and congressional situations and the difficulty in defining congressional conflict of interest.

SELF-DEALING BY A PUBLIC OFFICIAL

The implication of "self-dealing by a public official" is that public officials ought to disqualify themselves when a particular course of government action might significantly affect their personal economic interest. The difficulty with this notion when applied to the House of Representatives is that, unless congressmen are to have no source of income other than their salaries, it may be difficult for them to avoid situations that affect their own interests. A member of the executive branch charged with overseeing only one policy area may without undue hardship avoid personal holdings in that field. Congressmen cannot handle the problem that easily. As the late Senator Robert Kerr said, "If everyone abstained from voting on grounds of personal interest, I doubt if you could get a quorum in the United States Senate on any subject."[3]

In a recent study two researchers attempted to examine "as-

2. Roswell Perkins, "The New Federal Conflict of Interest Law," *Harvard Law Review*, vol. 26 (April 1963), pp. 1118–19.

3. Cited in Laurence Stern and Edwin Knoll, "Congress: When the Private Life of a Lawmaker Becomes a Public Affair," *Esquire*, April 1964, pp. 82–84.

sociations between the personal financial holdings of members of the Ninetieth Congress and their roll-call responses on votes relevant to those holdings."[4] They analyzed eleven fields of interest: finance, defense, the antiballistic missile system, farming, transportation, broadcasting, electrical power, law, airlines, petroleum, and capital gains. Although the authors found apparent correlations between personal holdings in an industry and pro-industry voting patterns in the case of electrical power and airlines, they found the opposite pattern in the case of farming, transportation, capital gains, and petroleum. In general they discovered "few if any examples of self-serving in the U.S. House of Representatives."

The authors of the study did find differences between interested and disinterested members (those with or without relevant financial holdings) with respect to the size of winning coalitions. Members with relevant financial holdings showed a tendency to favor those holdings in close votes and were more likely than others to change their votes when a compromise alternative was offered. The authors pointed out in addition that "record votes on the floor are but a small part of the total legislative process" and that there may be errors in their findings because overly stringent standards may have caused them to overlook potentially interesting results. Furthermore, there may have been shortcomings in the financial data available or in the nature of the inquiry itself.

On the other hand, the findings may be accurate. As another observer has commented: "In the ordinary ranges of stock ownership the rewards from favoritism or worse are simply inadequate. The official runs all the risks of detection and obloquy but receives only one-thousandth or one-millionth of the proceeds. Even a narrow, grasping man will find this disproportion

4. James W. Lindeen and Shirley A. Lindeen, "Conflict of Interest in the U.S House of Representatives: Some Preliminary Findings" (paper delivered at the Annual Meeting of the Midwest Political Science Association in Chicago, May 1973).

between risks and profits uninviting."[5] The benefits a congressman might get from favoring his stock holdings are not worth
the risks he runs. A congressman risks less if he favors an interest for other deferred compensation such as future employment, which we will discuss later. In addition, a legislator's
vote in favor of a certain stock holding may also benefit his
constituents (depending on how they are defined). Group 6
questionnaire items, which are given in table 3-1, touched on
these issues.

According to the responses, congressmen believe that it is a
common practice for their colleagues to promote personal interests that coincide with constituent interests. Item 3, for example, in which a legislator owning $100,000 worth of savings
and loan stock votes for a tax amendment favoring the savings
and loan industry, was the most disapproved item in this group,
presumably because of the size of the stock holding, yet the
respondents did not believe that disapproval would prevent
such behavior on the part of their colleagues. In general these
questionnaire responses support the interview conclusions that
congressmen are not particularly worried about promoting personal interests that coincide with constituent interest.

One potential conflict of private and public interest occurs
when congressmen devote a significant amount of time to personal business interests. To the extent that time spent promoting a personal fortune could otherwise be spent on public
business, the public is the loser and there is a conflict between
their interest and that of their representative.

Outside business interests do present unnecessary and avoid-
able conflicts, but congressmen disagree widely about their
legitimacy. There are three distinct opinions in Congress about
such interests: that any time spent away from congressional
business is improper; that although outside income is desirable,
law practice is very conflict prone; and that outside business is

5. George Stigler, "The Economics of Conflict of Interest," *The Journal
of Political Economy*, vol. 75 (February 1967), pp. 100–101.

Table 3-1. *Mean Scores on Questionnaire Items, Group 6: Promoting Personal Interests that Coincide with Constituent Interests*

	Mean score	
Questionnaire item	*Judgment of practice*[a]	*Extent of practice*[b]
(3) A legislator owns $100,000 worth of stock in a hometown savings and loan association and votes in favor of an amendment to a tax bill that benefits the savings and loan industry as a whole.	2.28	2.24
(37) A legislator owns 2,000 acres of cotton-producing land. He represents a constituency in which cotton is the major agricultural crop. He receives an assignment to the Committee on Agriculture where he actively works for higher price supports for cotton.	2.48	2.23
(38) A legislator is president of a local labor union. He wins election to Congress and is granted a two-year leave by his union executive board, which continues his pension and retirement rights. He is appointed to the committee with jurisdiction over labor matters. He works actively for repeal of the right-to-work laws and less restrictive federal controls over labor organizations.	2.56	2.20
(2) A legislator owns $5,000 worth of stock in a hometown savings and loan association and votes in favor of an amendment to a tax bill that benefits the savings and loan industry as a whole.	2.65	1.74

a. Scoring for judgment of practice:
    1 = clearly unethical   3 = probably ethical
    2 = probably unethical   4 = clearly ethical
b. Scoring for extent of practice:
    1 = most congressmen   3 = few
    2 = many   4 = none

acceptable, including law practice, which is no different from any other business and should not to be discriminated against. One northeastern Republican put the first case forcefully.

People invariably think of a conflict of financial interest, but the conflict in time is more important. Unless you give to the job all your time and energy, I think you have a conflict of interest. When I see it, it bothers me as I know I need between seventy and seventy-five hours a week to do this job. I just don't think a member should have outside professional and business interests.

A western Democrat exemplified the second position.

I have to maintain outside interests. What if I'm defeated tomorrow? What do I do? My business might be a fiction, but I keep it like a security blanket. It's something that I might have to use. I think the big problem is the lawyer/legislator. If I did what they do, I could be put in prison.

This critique was echoed by a southern Democrat.

The biggest criticism I can see is those attorneys who maintain an active law practice. A large percentage of that practice is generated because of their position in Congress. They are also the active members of the Tuesday-to-Thursday Club. If we could get them to come down here and work a five-day week, why we would be done with our work three months earlier.

Despite what several lawyer members saw as an apparent injustice in condemning law practice while allowing other business interests, many other members felt quite strongly that law ties presented special difficulties. As one western Democrat said bluntly: "The similarity of legal practice and congressional behavior is so close that it is an obvious channel for sanitized bribery and influence peddling. Every major bribery effort of a public official goes through a law firm." "Double door" law firms with one "door" listing a congressman's name as a partner (for the nonfederal business) and another eliminating his name (for federal business) were often unfavorably mentioned.

Both of the positions above—that of abstaining totally from outside occupations and that of prohibiting only law practice —were disputed by several lawyer members. As a southern Democrat put it:

I think a member should have an outside interest. The worst single mistake I made, besides probably running for Congress, was to give up my law practice. I think you need—at least I need—an adequate income to support a family when you have several children in college at one time as I do.

Other members cited another important reason for maintaining an outside occupation and income. "I could survive without having a law firm partnership," one said, "but I think having the partnership gives me a feeling of independence as to what I do here. Otherwise my future will be up to the whims of local party officials." This argument also applies to independence from special interests. As a northern Republican noted:

I think that if you have a business or income connection, you can be very much more independent as a member of Congress. If you're defeated, you can go back to your profession. If you're a professor, you can get a job in a university. If you have nothing to go back to, why you may become more dependent and less independent.

Several members said that a legislator from a rural area may have more time to pursue an outside interest than one from an active urban district may have. The time conflict was not seen as much of a problem if, in fact, a member's district did not put time demands on him. This position overlooks the possibility that a member less pressed by constituent demands could spend more time on substantive legislative business. Nevertheless, several members did make the distinction.

Disapproval of an active outside law practice and the recognition of certain extenuating circumstances are both revealed in the questionnaire responses to group 7 (table 3-2). In their responses to questions about ties with law firms, congressmen recognized the ethical problems an active law practice can entail, or even encourage. They also recognized, however, that a junior congressman who may not be reelected should not have to cut himself off from his legal career. The respondents saw a difference between a congressman who simply maintains ties with his law firm and one who allows his law firm to profit from his congressional service. They considered the questionnaire item (35) in which a newly elected legislator and his law firm appear to benefit from his membership on the Commerce Committee to be a fairly common practice, although they judged it to be unethical.

Judging from the responses to the questions in this study, congressmen are unlikely to voluntarily limit the range of outside activities open to them. There is a widespread feeling in Congress that outside business interests (with the possible exception of a law practice) are legitimate and necessary, either for personal financial security or for legislative independence. Coupled with the unwillingness of congressmen to interfere with their colleagues' personal habits or relations with their constituents, these attitudes protect even law affiliation. The difficulty of regulating one particular activity, which will certainly be considered unfair discrimination by those most affected, makes it unlikely that outside law practice will be formally prohibited.

The act of prohibiting law practice would draw attention to the entire range of outside congressional business interests and the attendant real or imagined abuses. Members of Congress prefer not to publicize congressional misbehavior or the suspicion of it. Time after time, the congressmen in our sample acknowledged this tendency, saying, "We presume the constituency will take care of it," or "A guy's finances are his own business" (provided always that the "guy" does not bring Congress as a whole into disrepute).

Table 3-2. *Mean Scores on Questionnaire Items, Group 7:*
Ties with Law Firms

Questionnaire item	Mean score	
	Judgment of practice[a]	Extent of practice[b]
(35) A newly elected legislator from a marginal district is not sure that he will be reelected and is reluctant to sever his partnership in a major law firm. He is assigned to the Commerce Committee, and subsequently a number of railroads, truck firms, and airlines request the firm to handle their problems before state and city bodies only. The legislator's partnership agreement provides that he will receive a share of the profits on this nonfederal business.	1.84	2.66
(36) A legislator requests that he no longer receive a share of his law firm's profits but agrees for prestige reasons to have his name continue to be listed on the letterhead, and in return the firm continues to provide substantial group life insurance coverage for him. His firm has both a federal and state regulatory practice.	2.56	2.25
(34) A newly elected legislator from a marginal district is not sure that he will be reelected and is reluctant to sever his partnership in a major law firm. He makes an arrangement with his partners so that he only receives a share of the profits on his nonfederal business.	3.14	1.95

a. Scoring for judgment of practice:
   1 = clearly unethical   3 = probably ethical
   2 = probably unethical   4 = clearly ethical
b. Scoring for extent of practice:
   1 = most congressmen   3 = few
   2 = many   4 = none

Pressure for restrictions on outside business interests and law practice must come from outside Congress. It is unrealistic to expect Congress to act unless there is public demand for change. One indication that public opinion may have some effect is seen in the dwindling number of congressmen continuing to maintain law practices in the last few years.

The number of House members practicing law dropped significantly in 1971. Sixty-six representatives reported earning $1,000 or more from their law practices in 1971, while eighty-one had done so in both 1969 and 1970. Only six lawyer members reported outside income in excess of $5,000 in 1971, compared with twenty-four in 1968, eleven in 1969, and nine in 1970.[6] The decline followed an American Bar Association (ABA) vote in 1969 critical of the practice of law by legislators. Nevertheless, this appeared to leave 58 of 232 House lawyers—one in four—either practicing part time or at least affiliated with a law firm. One member who continued to practice law said the ABA restriction amounted to "disbarring a man without the right of hearing; it is entirely out of order." The report of the National Committee for an Effective Congress on the financial disclosure data for 1972 indicated that law affiliations had fallen further, although the study covered only the 363 nonfreshmen members of the Ninety-third Congress, not the 72 members of the previous Congress who had been defeated, had retired, or had died.[7]

Another kind of pressure on the outside activities of congressmen came in November 1972 when the United States Court of Appeals for the District of Columbia upheld the finding of a federal district court that it is unconstitutional for members of Congress to hold commissions in ready, standby, or even retired status in the armed forces reserves. At that time 117 senators and representatives held such commissions, including members of the Armed Services committees and the subcommittees dealing with veterans affairs (which handle compensation and pensions). Yet congressmen in our sample gave a rating that fell between "probably" and "clearly" unethical to a questionnaire item in which a legislator asks for and receives

6. *Congressional Quarterly Report*, vol. 30 (June 17, 1972), p. 1383.
7. National Committee for an Effective Congress, "Analysis of 1972 House Financial Disclosure Reports" (Washington, D.C.: NCEC, June 3, 1973; processed).

an Army reserve commission while on the Armed Services Committee.

In the court test of reserve commissions, the circuit court upheld the lower court's opinion that a commission in the reserves amounts to an "office" under the meaning of Article 1, Section 6 of the Constitution, which states that "no person holding any office under the United States shall be a member of either House during his continuance in office." The plaintiffs (the Reservist Committee to Stop the War et al.) contended that a direct conflict of interest exists when congressmen vote to increase military pay and benefits which they then draw themselves. The Justice Department appealed the matter to the Supreme Court, which reversed the lower courts on the grounds that the plaintiffs had no standing to sue.

Outside pressure against the reserve commissions has been less effective than pressure against law practices, but congressional membership in the reserves is declining. At the beginning of the Ninety-third Congress in 1973, 106 members of both houses held reserve commissions, including House Speaker Carl Albert. At the start of the Ninety-fourth Congress, only ninety-five legislators, still including Albert, held commissions.

DISCRETIONARY TRANSFER OF ECONOMIC VALUE

The most extreme form of discretionary transfer of economic value from a private source to a public official—the second area of possible conflict—is bribery, which is illegal. There are many less extreme forms, however, that also raise questions.

Even in cases of demonstrated bribery, the congressional situation is unique. Congressmen are protected under the Constitution from arrests in civil suits and for words written or spoken in the execution of their office. Former Congressman John Dowdy of Texas was convicted of bribery, conspiracy, and perjury in a case involving the protection of a home improvement firm accused of fraud. In April 1973 an appeals court overturned the bribery and conspiracy convictions. The court did not find that Dowdy was innocent of the acts charged;

rather it ruled that his acts could be interpreted as being in the line of his duty on a subcommittee and as such would be protected legislative acts, even if he was being bribed to so act.[8] The perjury conviction was left standing.

In 1963 the conviction of Congressman Thomas L. Johnson of Maryland on charges of receiving a bribe in exchange for giving a speech on the House floor was also overturned on these constitutional grounds. Johnson's speech, extolling savings and loan institutions, was reprinted and distributed by officers of a Maryland savings and loan company then under indictment. (Congressman Frank Boykin of Alabama, who was also convicted in the case, paid a fine of $10,000 and did not appeal. He was later pardoned by President Johnson.) Congressman Johnson was later convicted for a second time on federal conflict of interest charges and was sentenced to six months in prison.

The difficulties of trying to regulate behavior such as Johnson's floor speech are enormous. To be able to convict Johnson on the basis of his speech would jeopardize, for example, a member from an urban district who received large campaign contributions from labor interests and subsequently gave a speech in the House favorable to those interests. The latter is an example of legitimate political behavior and the promotion of constituency interests, as well as a common method of rewarding contributors.

Two questionnaire items (group 5) dealt with inserting speeches or other material in the *Congressional Record* on behalf of contributors. Respondents considered performing such a service for a contributor outside the district less proper than performing it for a constituent, but both practices were deemed not uncommon (see table 3-3).

Many other unique circumstances surrounding congressional rewards from private sources blur the charge of conflict of in-

8. Article 1, Section 6 of the Constitution protects legislators against being "questioned in any other place" for legislative acts. This is commonly referred to as the "speech or debate" clause.

Table 3-3. *Mean Scores on Questionnaire Items, Group 5: Insertions in* Congressional Record *Favoring Campaign Contributors*

	Mean score	
Questionnaire item	Judgment of practice[a]	Extent of practice[b]
(29) A legislator has a number of substantial industrial and labor contributors from *outside his constituency* who provide him with a large amount of his campaign funds. During the session, the legislator puts one or two articles or speeches about each industrial and labor organization in the *Congressional Record* as his way of thanking them for their support.	2.24	2.38
(28) A legislator has ten contributors from different industries and labor organizations in his constituency who raise most of his campaign funds. During the session, the legislator puts one or two articles or speeches about each industry and labor organization in the *Congressional Record* as his way of thanking them for their support.	2.52	2.28

a. Scoring for judgment of practice:
    1 = clearly unethical   3 = probably ethical
    2 = probably unethical   4 = clearly ethical
b. Scoring for extent of practice:
    1 = most congressmen   3 = few
    2 = many   4 = none

terest. Just as no laws forbid congressmen to engage in outside business activity, none forbid them to accept honorariums, although legislation in 1974 limited payments for each speech or article to $1,000 and the total annual income from such activities to $15,000. Legislators commonly receive stipends for speaking before private groups, including those concerned with legislation before their committees. Two questionnaire items addressed this issue. One asked about a member who accepted a $1,000 honorarium from a group with which he had long been identified. The other asked about a member who accepted the same sum from a group, new to him, that was interested in upcoming legislation, while he was undecided how to vote on the issue. The respondents deemed the first situation probably ethical and widely practiced. They considered the second more unethical (mean: 1.84, where 1 = clearly unethical and 2 = probably unethical) but also fairly likely to be practiced (mean: 2.71, where 2 = many and 3 = few).

Honorariums can be treated as direct income. They are an obvious, and for many a very lucrative, discretionary transfer of economic value to a public official. Campaign contributions are a different matter. Nevertheless, they fall in the same category and may present many of the same conflicts.

Members of the House of Representatives must run for re-election every two years. In a closely contested district the costs of a primary and general campaign may run over $100,000. A congressman earning less than half that sum a year could not hope to manage such expenses on his own, and he is not expected to. He can use his salary and associated allowances to partially support his campaign, but he must raise a campaign fund to meet the bulk of his expenses. Although the amounts of money needed in an election campaign and the methods employed for raising funds vary greatly among members, the funds all come from the private sector.

Campaign funds and personal finances may complement each other, with an unclear line between expenses that should be charged to one or the other. Unexpended campaign funds can be used for political as opposed to personal expenses between campaigns. However, if a congressman does not have unused campaign funds, he pays for political expenses vital to his performance (or continuance) in office out of his own pocket. Many respondents reported that they used considerable amounts of their own funds to run their offices and to serve their constituents.

In addition to the trips that congressmen are authorized to take to their districts at government expense each year, they

Table 3-4. *Mean Scores on Questionnaire Items, Group 2: Personal Use of Campaign Funds*

	Mean score	
Questionnaire item[a]	Judgment of practice[b]	Extent of practice[c]
(24) Expanding the den in his home in the constituency to serve as his headquarters when Congress is not in session.	1.40	3.10
(20) Travel cost of the legislator's wife who accompanies him on a study mission to Europe.	1.45	2.95
(15) A legislator's wife is a skilled campaigner. She travels weekly with her husband to visit the constituency. So that she can look fresh and up-to-date, her husband buys her three new dresses each month and charges them to his campaign fund.	1.72	2.93
(27) Buying a second car to leave in the constituency so that he will be able to travel about when he flies in from Washington.	2.00	2.98
(21) Travel cost of the legislator's wife, who accompanies him on visits to the constituency.	2.14	2.61
(26) Paying the dues of a Washington social club so that he will have a nice place to entertain constituents.	2.20	2.63

a. All items except number 15 refer to the following hypothetical situation: A legislator instructs his administrative assistant to manage and raise the funds for his reelection campaign. After the campaign is over, 25 percent of the campaign funds remain unspent. The legislator has his administrative assistant set up a checking account and tells him to use the funds to pay the cost of the items given above. Respondents were asked to pass judgment on the appropriateness of paying these items from an office expense fund.

b. Scoring for judgment of practice:
    1 = clearly unethical   3 = probably ethical
    2 = probably unethical   4 = clearly ethical

c. Scoring for extent of practice:
    1 = most congressmen   3 = few
    2 = many   4 = none

can use unexpended campaign funds to pay for additional trips home by including one political function. By visiting the district office, meeting with supporters, or addressing a local organization, a congressman can claim that the trip was political and charge it to excess funds, whether he spends most of the time at leisure with his family or not.

The respondents agreed that the use of campaign funds for activities that bear little relation to any campaign is improper. Group 2 questionnaire items, shown in table 3-4, asked for judgments on the personal use of campaign funds. The responses clearly reveal congressional disapproval of improper diversion of campaign money. When the activity in question has more to do with constituency service, congressmen approve it more. This pattern appeared often in this study and indicates distinctions that should be considered in reform proposals. Because campaign finance raises so many questions, we will deal with it at much greater length in chapter 4.

In the interviews, we asked questions about the extent to which congressmen would accept special favors from lobbyists. Specific questions referred to lobbyists paying the entertainment costs of legislators or lending them planes for personal travel or campaign purposes. Other questions dealt with the leasing or selling of automobiles to legislators at substantial discounts and the provision of free hotel rooms in the legislators' districts.

Overall, the congressmen saw very little wrong in most of these practices. Many reported that lobbyists had never paid for entertainment for groups of constituents or for political gatherings; others mentioned that it happened once in a while or that they had been to parties that were probably paid for by private interests. Those who recognize the practice were not particularly upset by it, believing it to be a legitimate campaign-associated activity.

The practice of using private planes for personal travel or campaigning also raised few eyebrows. Slightly less than half of the sample admitted to using planes that had been put at their disposal, although the majority stated that they did so occasionally rather than frequently. More than 10 percent of the sample, however, said that they used such planes often. Only a small number of congressmen said such activity was wrong. A western Republican said he was "wary of the practice," and a midwestern Republican said he considered it "questionable," but many others who did not report using private planes said this practice was inconvenient or unnecessary. (One southern legislator reported simply, "I don't go home.")

A midwestern Republican gave a typical response to a question about using airplanes belonging to others: "I think these planes come in handy. Nobody ever tried to collect from me because they hauled me around to a speech. Firms in my area do it for the Democratic senator and the national committeeman as well as myself." Another Republican from a border state agreed. "I don't think there is any real problem on this. I don't think anybody really expects anything. You are just one person on a committee, and unless you are the chairman I don't see how you can be too much help to them."

Most congressmen in the sample looked upon the provision of planes as a convenience that they would be foolish to ignore and as the sort of activity that does not create difficult bonds or debts. One eastern Republican who did not engage in the practice said, "I really can't think why I haven't done it, since I would do anything for the company anyhow because they're in my constituency." He added, however, "I guess it would look bad if I did take a ride on the plane." A large proportion of his colleagues did not agree. Much more common were comments such as this one from a western Democrat: "I was offered a trip on a DC-6, but it would take a week across the country in a DC-6. Both [major air frame companies] that have plants in my district made the offer. I turned it down for inconvenience. I don't think it's any problem."

Scarcely any congressmen thought it was wrong to accept free hotel rooms in their districts. Many reported that they enjoyed such benefits and considered it perfectly legitimate behavior. Many others said they did not receive such treatment and wished they did. A number of congressmen mentioned that it was possible to offend a constituent by refusing the offer of a hotel room or a complimentary dinner in a restaurant.

Many members thought that it was improper to accept discounts on car leases. One reported that he used to get the free use of a car from one of the major auto companies but that he "certainly cut it out once the Dodd case happened."[9] Even though they disapproved, members knew of such arrangements, indicating that the practice was not completely rejected. In several cases the main complaint was that the discounts were a privilege reserved only for committee chairmen. "I told a friend of mine in Congress who has such an arrangement to send the person around, but he never came by. I'd certainly like to take advantage of it," one legislator said.

We asked the congressmen if they participated in inaugural airline trips. (An inaugural trip takes place when an airline opens service to a new location. The airline invites dignitaries on the initial flight. This can constitute a free vacation.) Very few saw anything wrong with accepting the trip. On the contrary, most members believed that travel helped them in their work by contributing to their understanding of world conditions. No one was offended by the junketing aspect of the trips, although several admitted to that dimension. A typical comment was:

I don't think it's a problem. I found it very helpful. I went to India on a TWA flight. I had never been there. We spent ten days there and I learned much more about India than I had ever known before. TWA has never asked me for a thing, and now I hear from our ambassador there all the time, and I have a better understanding of the country.

Others stated that they had not taken trips, but in the words

9. Senator Thomas Dodd's censure by the Senate is discussed in chapter 1.

of one: "It's been a matter of time, not ethics. I think it would be a good thing." Another noted: "I've never been invited on any and I regret it. It's all very disillusioning never to have been asked."

In a general discussion of government-paid travel by congressmen that grew out of the inaugural flight questions, most respondents said that much work did get done on the trips and that the diligent members on study/work trips well outnumbered those along for pleasure. Work and relaxation may enjoy a peaceful coexistence, however, as one comment demonstrates:

I can remember when I was on the Agriculture Committee, the committee was going to Europe to investigate Public Law 480, and I found out they were taking two of the best-looking secretaries along who weren't necessarily the most competent. I protested to the chairman and told him that either they stayed home or I did. The result was that I stayed home.

Despite such reports, most of the congressmen resented the "junketing" label given to congressional travel and the skeptical attitude taken by many journalists. They felt that press stories often create unfair public bias against travel that damages hard-working members who seriously need to learn the effects of American policies abroad or to witness firsthand the practices and conditions in other nations. Former Speaker Sam Rayburn's boast that he had never been outside the United States was often cited by the congressmen as indicative of an unfortunate parochialism, not far removed from xenophobia.

The questionnaire responses supported many of the findings from the interviews but also revealed a number of practices that were considered improper. These responses are enlightening because they clearly indicate that congressmen can and do differentiate between legitimate and less legitimate conduct (table 3-5).

A questionnaire item that did not group statistically with

the rest dealt with another kind of favor from private interests, and received the following response:

	Mean score	
	---	---
Questionnaire item	Judgment of practice	Extent of practice
(14) Plays poker with lobbyists interested in his committee and wins consistently.	1.79	2.83

The congressmen in the sample seemed to consider accepting favors from outside interests less ethical than receiving favors from constituents, special favors less ethical than routine ones, and favors of cash less ethical than ones of service. Such distinctions show possible directions for future reform.

A common although initially surprising finding was that lobbyists paid little or no attention to many members. "As I said, I have never had a lobbyist take me to lunch and I'm frankly amazed, because it is different in my state legislature," was a common refrain. Those members who had served in state legislatures before being elected to Congress believed that standards of conduct were much lower in the state capitals than in Washington.

The apparently higher standard at the national level is not simply due to the fact that the greater responsibility or the year-round term of a national legislature brings out the best in its members or to the fact that there is much more probing and sophisticated journalistic coverage of Washington politics. One reason for the higher level of conduct may be that the average member of Congress is ordinarily not worth as much to a lobbyist as the average member of a state legislature is. The House is a large and in many ways unwieldy body. The division of labor into committees and subcommittees that takes place in all legislatures is much greater in the 435-member House of Representatives than in, say, the 100-member Senate. House members usually serve on only one major committee, but in the

Table 3-5. *Mean Scores on Questionnaire Items, Group 3: Favors from Private Interests*

	Mean score	
Questionnaire item	Judgment of practice[a]	Extent of practice[b]
(8) A member of a national trade association calls on a new member of Congress and indicates that if he needs any funds because of the added expenses of moving to Washington he can arrange a loan with the legislator's local bank at substantially below the going rate of interest. The legislator agrees.	1.21	3.00
(32) A legislator serving on the Commerce and Government Operations committees, with jurisdiction over the automobile industry and the federal safety program, leases a new car each year from a major automobile manufacturer at half the cost at which the car is made available to business clients.	1.53	2.80
(12) A national firm with no plant in the legislator's constituency makes available at no charge its private plane and pilot whenever the legislator has speaking commitments in his state.	1.72	2.66
(9) A national hotel chain indicates to the legislator that any time he is home visiting his constituency he is welcome to have a free room or suite with the compliments of the house. The legislator accepts the offer and utilizes the complimentary facilities several weeks each year.	1.79	2.59
(31) A legislator, not on a committee dealing with automobile safety or automobile industry regulation, leases a new car each year from a major automobile manufacturer at half the cost at which the car is made available to business clients.	1.88	2.54

Table 3-5. *Continued*

Questionnaire item	Mean score	
	Judgment of practice[a]	Extent of practice[b]
(11) A major industry located in the constituency makes available at no charge its private plane and pilot whenever the legislator has speaking commitments in the state.	2.00	2.51
(10) A local hotel makes a complimentary room or suite available to the representative and two senators from a state when they are in the area. The legislators utilize the complimentary facilities several weeks each year. One of the senators is a Democrat; the other is a Republican.	2.28	2.35
(13) A leading firm in the legislator's constituency has a private plane which regularly flies between Washington and a city near the legislator's home. The legislator is told that there is always extra space if he wants a free ride home on Friday afternoons, and he uses the plane fairly frequently.	2.53	2.20

a. Scoring for judgment of practice:
    1 = clearly unethical   3 = probably ethical
    2 = probably unethical   4 = clearly ethical
b. Scoring for extent of practice:
    1 = most congressmen   3 = few
    2 = many   4 = none

U.S. Senate and in many state legislatures it is normal to serve on two, three, or even more committees. As a consequence, House members feel more remote from much of the legislation and from even the daily operations of Congress.

This point is not inconsistent with that made elsewhere that there is little party control in the House and that pressures to vote a certain way are often ineffective. Committee chairmen in the House wield great power over both the content and the process of legislation, a power that is often more important than the ability to dictate a member's final vote.

With respect to the third possible conflict under consideration—public officials giving assistance to private parties dealing with the government—the dilemma caused by the demands of the legislator's role is immediately apparent. Constituents expect most congressmen to offer assistance in dealing with a huge and seemingly unresponsive government, and legislators view such service as vital to reelection.

The fourth possible conflict can occur when former public officials give assistance to private parties dealing with the government. Again the situations of congressmen and executive branch personnel are different. The latter presumably could offer special access to government deliberations only in the field (and indeed perhaps only in the bureau) in which they had been previously employed. Thus to legislate a required period during which they could not deal with the bureau that had formerly employed them would be neither difficult nor excessively discriminatory. Congress, however, is not a bureau. A comparable prohibition would debar former members from lobbying Congress itself. Yet to prohibit retired or defeated members from such practice might be discriminatory. Moreover, the potential for the misuse of an executive official's knowledge of contemplated administrative actions has few parallels on the legislative side.

In any case, members are unlikely to vote such a restriction. Some of them look upon the possibility of service as a Washington representative as a form of insurance. The legislative process is what they know best. To preclude congressmen from this field would be unfair in their view.

In a related area, members of Congress were asked about the extent and effectiveness of former legislators serving as lobbyists, particularly because of their access to the House floor. The general response was that, with certain exceptions, ex-legislator lobbyists did not abuse their privileges. Several members noted that the floor is not a good place to lobby because members often leave the floor quickly when they are not needed so that they can attend to other responsibilities.

Ex-legislator lobbyists do have one advantage. Congressmen often listen to former members because of their continuing friendships or because the ex-members "know the ropes." These lobbyists ask about conditions "out in the district" and know enough not to embarrass a member. Ex-congressmen in general make effective lobbyists—but not because of their access to the floor. A western representative observed that they have "a definite advantage. They know what goes on; they have a feel for the Hill. They have an interest in your problems." Another westerner noted, "As a new member, you are particularly impressed by the attention you get from former members who are lobbyists."

Only in the last of the five suggested conflicts of interest—deriving private gain from the use of information acquired in an official capacity—is the situation of a congressman similar to that of a nonelected official. Clearly congressmen should refrain from using inside information. It is as improper for them to use information gained from executive sessions of a committee as it is for a member of a regulatory commission to do so. Because congressmen deal with many issues, however, they might consider themselves a special case and believe that they should not be prohibited from using inside information. But the organization of Congress, with its division of labor through the committee system, generally limits a congressman's access to useful inside information to those activities that come under the jurisdiction of his committee. Requesting a congressman to refrain from dealing in those specific matters would not constitute the same penalty as a more generalized prohibition. This might also prove a satisfactory way of limiting lobbying by ex-congressmen.

When we questioned congressmen about using information obtained in executive sessions of a committee for private gain, few of them cited evidence of members benefiting from such information. The responses were quite uniform: "There isn't much opportunity really—if you read the *Washington Post* you know as much as we do," or "You'd have to really hustle out of the committee room to have it work," or "There are a lot easier ways of getting rich around here if you really want to cheat." Congressmen generally suggest that rewards from committee assignments, if there are any, come in other forms. As one said, "I think you get a lot more of this in terms of campaign contributions."

This impression was sustained by the responses to a questionnaire item on this issue. The respondents rated this activity the *least* ethical of all the hypothetical situations (mean = 1.16; 1 = clearly unethical) and there was little variation in the judgment. The respondents were equally convinced that few members would engage in the practice (mean = 3.00, or few).

Disclosure: The Simple Answer?

Disclosure of personal financial details, the most commonly suggested solution to traditional conflict of interest problems, is a troublesome and often painful topic for congressmen. Many recognize the problems of potential conflict of interest and the legitimate request of constitutents either to be assured that their votes are not permitting congressmen to enrich themselves or to have an adequate opportunity to learn if such is the case. But congressmen believe they should have the same rights to privacy and to the pursuit of wealth that other Americans have. A typical comment, although more colorful than most, was made by an eastern Democrat.

I am violently against disclosure, not just because I am a member of Congress, but because I'm an individual. I'm involved in business with a group of people who own land in my district, and this has nothing to do with the government. I have two or three pieces of land with friends. I don't think this is anybody's business. Why should I disclose? If I do, it will give competitors of ours an edge. We don't work for the government. We're citizens and individuals in public office. The concept of a member of Congress is not to be a test-tube creation with no interests. We are citizens in office sent by the people back home. If we screw up once, we're going to be out of office.

Another congressman added: "I'm especially disturbed about filing the disclosure statement when my opponent doesn't have to do it, and neither does the state senator from my area or any member of the school board. If everybody had to file a disclosure statement, OK, I would support it, but I don't want to be alone."

In the interviews the congressmen pointed to several other problems with disclosure. The primary problem was that disclosure might discourage qualified, capable, honest candidates from running for office.

Limited financial disclosures are now required of congressmen under House Rule 44. The first such reports were due April 30, 1969, for the calendar year 1968. House Rule 44 requires the submission of a two-part report. Part A, which is available for "responsible public inquiry," requires a member to "list the name, instrument of ownership and any position of management held in any business entity doing a substantial business with the Federal Government or subject to Federal regulatory agencies, in which the ownership is in excess of $5,000 fair market value as of the date of filing or from which income of $1,000 or more was derived during the preceding calendar year."[10] Members are not required to list the dollar

10. House Rule 44 also requires listing the name, address, and type of practice of any professional organization in which the person reporting, or his spouse, is an officer or serves in an advisory capacity and from which income of $1,000 or more was derived during the preceding year, and the source of any income for services rendered exceeding $5,000, any capital gain from a single source (excepting sale of residence occupied by the person reporting) and any reimbursement for expenditures exceeding $1,000. The

values of any of these interests. Part B does require a listing of the fair market value of holdings and the dollar amount of income included in part A. Part B cannot be made public, however. It is sealed and filed with the Committee on Standards of Official Conduct until such time as that committee "pursuant to its investigative authority, determines by a vote of not less than seven members of the Committee that the examination of such information is essential in an official investigation."

Analysts have pointed out several problems in using the information in part A to measure personal financial interests. The value of the business holdings a member has to own before he is required to disclose the holdings is high. The value refers to involvement in one firm, not to a sum of investments in a given area. A member could have several holdings just below the $5,000 level in various firms in the same field that add up to a substantial interest and yet not have to disclose any of the holdings. In addition, the rule does not define "substantial" business with the federal government, and it contains no enforcement measure.

Despite the apparent shortcomings of the present rule, the overall response of the members of Congress interviewed for this study to proposals for further regulation was negative. While disapproving total disclosure, the members recognized with reluctance that public demand might force them to accept it. Many members noted the difficulties in failing to disclose when their opponents do so. In this case, the opponent publicly challenges the incumbent, who cannot ignore the challenge without implying that he has something to hide.

---

rule was amended May 26, 1970 (effective January 1, 1971), to require the listing of any honorariums from a single source aggregating $300 and all creditors owed $10,000 or more during the preceding year for a period of ninety days or more, excepting indebtedness specifically secured by adequate assets. In each case no specific dollar values have to be attached to any of the disclosures. All that is required is a list of the sources of relevant income or indebtedness over the specified ceilings. The problems that can be encountered in gaining access to these data are described in *Congressional Quarterly Weekly Report*, vol. 27 (May 23, 1969), pp. 775–76.

The range of possible congressional conflicts of interest is considerable. At one extreme are the unavoidable conflicts. As one member observed:

Obviously, I have conflicts of interest in terms of Medicare, since I have a mother who is very old. I have a conflict of interest on education legislation since I have a little boy six months old. I have a conflict of interest on social security, since my mother is on it, and I'll eventually be on it.

Most Americans recognize the inevitability of such conflicts and do not expect congressmen to disqualify themselves from votes on these issues. In a representative system conflicts of this kind are bound to appear since the legislators are selected from the population they represent. But the other extreme, of course, is outright bribery.

Once outside the boundaries of bribery and overt self-dealing, there is very little consensus, at least among our respondents, about what constitutes a legitimate or an illegitimate business or political transaction. Several issues that we touched on briefly in this chapter deserve more intensive scrutiny. One of the most important is campaign financing. Yet it is difficult to determine propriety when a member represents a constituency that includes extensive enterprises from which he regularly receives campaign contributions in one form or another. Does this member vote for agriculture, for business, or for labor because these groups contribute to his campaign or because their interests are basic constituency interests? We turn to this issue next.

FOUR

The Special Case of Campaigning:
The Congressman and His Contributors

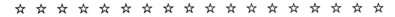

MOST OF OUR respondents recognized the dilemma posed by their need to raise campaign funds and their desire to maintain legislative independence. Nonetheless, when we asked what the members of our sample group thought most campaign contributors expect from a legislator and what the respondents regarded as the best way to raise campaign funds, their responses did not reflect a consensus. A number answered that most contributors expect nothing more than "good government," although one said:

Campaign finance creates an obligation and they know it. You tend to take the phone call from the heavy contributor more than from the unknown. And then there is the difference between doing something yourself for the heavy contributor or delegating it to a member of the staff.

Others said that contributors want contact with a congressman when they have an opinion to offer—that a contributor gets psychological satisfaction from being an insider. Some of the individual comments went as follows:

—*They expect an "ear." They expect "access." If they expect more, you shouldn't take their money.*

—*A lot of people like to be around politicians. They like to feel that they're "in," and they like you to tell them what's really going on inside. So I go out and meet them and tell them the inside things I get out of reading the Washington Post.*

—I think most contribute to me because they agree with my ways of doing things. In every case this is the way they can participate in good representative government. I'm brutally frank with them, and I'm as independent as a hog on ice. A number of contributors just like to be on the inside.

—I have been here eight years and to date nobody has called me and said, "Look, I've contributed to your campaign and I want this."

There were members, however, who admitted that certain contributors had baser motives; for example:

—I think most contributors are pretty good. At most, the ones that contribute to my campaign expect a little time with me during the course of the year and maybe a few want an actual quid pro quo. But most will leave you alone.

—The majority of my contributors are extreme idealists. They believe I'm fighting their battle to preserve the country. Of course, some are odds players and you'll get contributions of $500 or $1,000 every two years from these people who will never ask you for anything, but they're sort of making an investment so that if the big moment comes, old Jack will consider them his friend for all those years and help them. This is about 1 percent of the contributors. Then there's about 25 percent that just plain always help the incumbent. Then there's about 10 percent who simply get asked by your fund-raising committee and don't know how to turn you down.

It is not always the big contributors who expect prime treatment. One respondent commented: "The biggest contributors contact me the least. You can say as a general rule that the less they contribute the more they expect." On the other hand, another frequent comment was: "From what they give me, they can't be expecting very much." Probably because of the sensitivity of the issue, many congressmen reported that most campaign contributors expected no quid pro quo and that if they did, they would not get it.

The congressmen showed more variation in their judgment of the best way to raise campaign funds. The majority of those interviewed regarded fund raising as a constant and difficult task. Several congressmen stated that they relied on a few wealthy personal friends either to provide the funds or to collect what was needed from their acquaintances. Others said that they preferred many small contributions from a wide cross section of the constituency. Some said they depended primarily on large contributions from organized labor, and others reported that business or professional associations provided most of their funds.

Several members advocated fund-raising, or testimonial, dinners as the best way to raise money. Yet a southern Republican remarked: "We did hold a dinner, but this simply didn't work in my district. If the price is low enough, you get the faithful and don't raise much money. If the price is too high, the average man won't come." The respondents broke almost evenly between those who employ testimonial dinners and those who do not. Some thought the dinners were perfectly proper and quite effective, some thought them all right but not very useful, others thought them improper, and a few called them a form of blackmail. A typical comment was made by a member who held testimonial dinners: "I'll hold one dinner at maybe $25 or $50 a head and net about $15,000. A member of Congress just can't hold a $100-a-head dinner." Although most of the members reporting the use of testimonial dinners were Republicans, a conservative Republican offered one of the sharper comments about this activity: "It's a sort of blackmail situation when you get involved with these dinners," he said, "and the people that come have something to do with the committees on which you serve." A southern Democrat voiced similar misgivings: "Never. I'd sort of look askance at holding an appreciation luncheon or dinner. I'd hate to organize one for myself. I think it's so phony." A western Democrat had a more specific complaint: "I don't like those appreciation luncheons or functions held in the District of Columbia. They are mostly financed by various national organizations of business or labor lobbyists, and it's sort of a round robin of tapping."

The overall judgment of congressmen on testimonial dinners is difficult to determine. Republicans are apt to use testimonial dinners more than Democrats—probably because they are more successful for Republicans. A common evaluation by the Democrats was that the affairs were not improper but that they simply were ineffective. "Maybe 250 or 300 people will turn out and the net might only be $500, and it certainly takes a great amount of organization time." Republicans, too, have this problem.

One thousand and ninety people bought tickets and there were about 1,100 meals served. The caterer's charge alone was $4,651.84, and then the transportation cost to get the four members of Congress there, including the main speaker, was $1,283.12. The result was that we had $471.31 after all this trouble for each of our campaigns.

Other fund-raising techniques were mentioned. A southern Democrat stated, "The best way to raise the funds is to have a direct solicitation and mailing." But a New England Democrat preferred "small cocktail parties where a few friends get other friends together." The same man noted: "I'll probably talk to most of the people personally who will contribute to my campaign. I'll probably raise over half the funds I need by just getting on the telephone."

Very few were able to say, as did a southern Democrat, "I've been offered contributions, but I usually don't take any, because I have so little in campaign expenses. I just pay them out of my pocket." Some chose the informal technique of telephoning a few friends and having them call others. Some members sent out a selected mailing; others employed a blanket mailing. The single most common comment was "I've got a kind of unique arrangement." And one respondent added:

There is no best way [to raise funds]. It is scrounging around. I would rather take a beating in an alley than raise money for *my own campaign. I have a $10,000 deficit; if I lost, I would have a disaster in paying that off.*

Another member answered the question about the best way to raise funds with a single word—"begging."

How Much Is Enough?

Legislation passed in the fall of 1974 limits campaign contributions to any one candidate to $1,000 from individuals and $5,000 from organized groups in each primary, runoff, and general election. Individuals may not contribute a total of more than $25,000 annually in all federal elections. Organizations face no aggregate total limits nor any on contributions to party-affiliated groups.

That this is a response to Watergate revelations and not a reflection of congressional consensus is evident from this study. Congressmen were asked what was the largest campaign contribution they would accept. Many agreed with the standard voiced by a midwestern Republican: "Any gift over $1,000 should be examined with great care." Several members said that they would prefer to have smaller contributions and more of them in order to avoid any implication of indebtedness. Others, however, had no such qualms. A southern Democrat stated: "I have no limits. I've never had to worry about it getting that high. I'd like to have it get up to $10,000 a contribution. If somebody offered me it, I'd say, 'Hell, yes, I'll take it.'" A liberal eastern Democrat agreed. "I don't really have any limits on it. I'm eager to accept it if somebody wants to donate it."

Some respondents attempted to draw a distinction between receiving large contributions from close friends, a practice that was generally seen as perfectly proper, and receiving the same amounts from others. Several members said that $1,000 from a DuPont is no different from $25 from a farmer. Another member summarized his situation as follows:

To survive, I must spend at least $50,000 this year since it's a marginal district. I resent the implication that congressmen are evil-doers. They ought to limit the campaign period as the British do or put absolute limits on how funds are spent. To give unlimited countenance to unlimited conflict between candidates and then point the finger because something seems to lack propriety is too much. Things do happen; that's the nature of the game, and the game is so hot, and the competition is so bitter that you're often a victim of the American scene. I have six dailies, thirty-five weeklies, and fifteen radio stations in my area, and it costs money to communicate with these people.

Complaints about the parsimony of donors were common. For example, an eastern Democrat:

I was simply amazed at the vast number of businessmen that you would break your neck helping, and they wouldn't give you a penny for the campaign. We would get them contracts, we'd prevent government from closing plants that were filthy, and yet you got no help at campaign time. Not that we expected it . . . but!

A western Democrat:

I got about $1,000 from labor. They're a useless bunch. I doubt if we get three precinct workers out of the 500 that we have. They talk a lot and they posture around, but they're really a toothless lion.

A border state Republican:

The farmers will work for you, but you won't get any money out of them.

A midwestern Republican:

I got some help from the medical profession, but doctors don't contribute well; they are mostly a lot of talk.

An eastern Republican:

AMPAC [American Medical Political Action Committee] did help, but we're now apparently on the outs. One of the AMPAC leaders told the doctor in my district who was active in my campaign that I had turned out to be real sour as far as they were concerned since I was palling around with [two liberal Republicans]. These doctors are really funny, the way they figure out politics.

One solution to the problem of stingy contributors was provided by an eastern Democrat.

A few months ago the Washington vice-president of one of the merchant marine companies dropped in to see me to give me a check for $50. I told him he must be kidding. In fact, I phoned up the president of the company and figured they were in worse straits than I am if all they could afford was fifty bucks, and I told him frankly I didn't want anything to do with an outfit that would only produce $50 in a political campaign, and they'd better believe it after the election. And the result was that I got $200 out of them.

Despite the inconclusiveness of much of the campaign finance information, it is apparent that many campaigns cost a lot of money. For the most part, they are also more expensive than formally reported. More than one respondent said something similar to the western Republican who, in discussing his $45,500 costs from the most recent campaign noted: "This was lower than usual. The previous election, while I filed reports that said we spent $44,000, we really spent quite a bit more."

Legislation in the fall of 1974 also imposed spending ceilings of $70,000 for each primary, runoff, and general election for a seat in the House, allowing a small additional sum for fund raising. In states with primaries, this creates an effective ceiling of approximately $150,000. An examination of campaign expenditure data reported by the forty-three members of the Ninetieth Congress who filled out the questionnaire for this study revealed that seven reported total primary and general costs of over $100,000. One member reported a total cost of $200; another, $150,000. The average reported cost of a general election for each of the eighteen members of the sample with more than eight years' seniority was $23,000; that for the twenty-five members with four or less terms in Congress was $50,120. Costs for the eleven campaigns in the Northeast averaged $46,360. Twelve races in the West averaged $37,200; thirteen in the North Central States averaged $39,700, and seven races in the South averaged $27,700. Although the primaries in many southern states are often more important than the general elections, primary costs were much higher for candidates running in the Northeast and in the West than in the South. It is quite possible that the figures reported formally are considerably lower than actual expenditures. Undoubtedly campaign costs have risen since the Ninetieth Congress. Whether they have risen enough to make the $150,000 ceiling discriminatory to challengers (particularly in the Northeast) is unclear.

The Advantages of Incumbency

The congressmen in the study sample frequently referred to the advantages of incumbency in campaigns. A striking example was provided by a southern Democrat: "I spent about $200 last time. Ten years ago when I first ran against an incumbent I spent $40,000, but once I had won the primary and found I had no opposition in the general, I was all set." A western Democrat said much the same thing. "When I first ran for the seat, I had to compete in the primary and it cost me $90,000, but once I became the incumbent I never spent much more than $15,000." A first-term Republican from a North Central state reported expenditures of $60,000.

The district had been Republican for years. [The incumbent] probably hadn't spent much money, just went out to see a few friends every once in a while and got himself reelected. But [a Democrat] who beat him in 1964 because of the Goldwater debacle, did spend money and it became a marginal district, so in order to get the district away from him you had to spend that amount, since we knew that if he won a second term, he'd probably be in there forever.

In certain districts, challengers may face even greater problems, as evidenced by the comment of one southern Democrat. "I've got two Republicans who want to run against me the next time. One is a rich one, and I don't know what the other one is. Boy, will I fix them. I'm not going to fix them during the campaign, but I sure will fix them afterwards. They'll wish they'd never run against me."

One weapon of the incumbent is free postage under the frank. Several members recalled the advice of Sam Rayburn, an old political pro. As one said, "I guess it was Speaker Rayburn who once said that you should vote with the committee and use your mailing frank if you want to get along and be reelected to Congress." Members admit that the nature of much that is sent out under the frank is "political" rather than "legislative" and freely state that the frank represents a tremendous advantage to an incumbent in an election. A western Republican said:

Of course there is a political advantage to the incumbent, and there is probably abuse in the use of the frank, and I probably abuse it as much as any other member.

A western Democrat:

This letter I'm sending out right now to the new voters that have been added to my district—it's a political mailing, yet disguised as wanting to render service to new constituents added from a Republican member's district.

A midwestern Republican:

I think it's a real problem, especially when you're putting out your newsletter. I stay in the nonpolitical approach, but certainly issuing a newsletter is a political act.

Congressmen also receive a stationery and postage allowance, which can be paid in cash or services. Some members thought their colleagues were tempted to take the allowance in cash, use the frank for all mail, and convert the allowance to other political or personal purposes. One noted that the "nonpolitical" regulations on the frank were very difficult to follow since "being a member of Congress permeates your whole life. What part is congressional, and what part isn't?" The frank provides a political advantage that some members may be a bit embarrassed or guilty about, but they are unlikely to give it up.

Committees and Contributions

The congressmen were asked which standing committees were most advantageous to their members from the standpoint of fund raising. Again answers varied widely. "I really don't know" was a common response as was "Not mine, that's for sure." Five or six claimed that the question came as a real surprise; that they'd never thought about it before. The resigned comment of a New England Democrat, "I wish I knew," was repeated often in one form or another. Many congressmen, however, thought they knew which committees were good for fund raising. They often responded by naming the committee most relevant to their constituencies' interests—an understandable approach to the question but one that once again resulted in wide disparities in the answers.

A Democrat stated the obvious: "I think that any group that deals with a particular committee is more sensitive to that committee." Support for this interpretation lies in the fact that members of the Agriculture, Public Works, Banking and Currency, and Interstate and Foreign Commerce committees ranked them best for fund raising, while members of the

District of Columbia, Science and Astronautics, and Merchant Marine committees rated their committees second best.

Often, however, members cited a committee on which they did not sit as good for contributions, while members who did sit on that committee judged it of little help. This was true of the Judiciary, Interior, and Education and Labor committees. A member of the Merchant Marine Committee also ranked it low, although another member placed it second. Many members suggested that Armed Services or Science and Astronautics must be good because of the likelihood of defense contract money. To this a western Republican responded:

I don't see it. I support our defense policy, and I hardly ever see any defense contractors. [An executive of a major defense supplier] in my area thinks that a $50 contribution is doing me a real favor and [a voluntary defense contractor employee political fund] gave me all of about $2 and some cents in the last campaign.

A western Democrat, however, reported: "My money really comes from the people I've helped, and of course I've helped the space companies. [An executive of an aerospace firm] is helpful. I haven't heard from [another aerospace firm] yet, but they will offer me more than I need." Perhaps these differences in viewpoint also reflect the power available to committee members of the majority party that is not available to the minority.

Several members of the Post Office and Civil Service Committee thought it was valuable for fund raising, but a western Democrat stated, "It's supposed to be one of those committees, but I don't believe it." A Republican member of the important Appropriations Committee noted: "It's powerful, but it doesn't really bring in campaign money as such. I think to get campaign funds you have to be a member of the majority party, have seniority, and be influential." Perhaps the most balanced statement was made by a midwestern Republican.

I am not too impressed that just by being on a committee you are more likely to get campaign funds. I think if you are an outstanding legislator you are likely to get on one or more com-

mittees, and the people will then think you are a policymaker and they'll loosen their pocketbooks at campaign time. And I really wonder how lucrative membership on a committee would be in terms of the total cost of your campaign. We're talking about a lot of money to wage a campaign in a metropolitan district. You certainly wouldn't get it from any one group in terms of what your needs are.

A representative who had previously played an active role in a major state legislature said: "The House of Representatives is completely different from the state legislature. Here in Washington I hardly ever see a lobbyist. They don't seem to talk to anybody but the chairman of the committee and the committee staff." Many members complained of the difficulties associated with campaign fund raising and mentioned something to the effect that "the chairman got $5,000, but they only gave me $200." As another western member observed at the close of an interview, "I think you have to be at least a subcommittee chairman, if not a committee chairman, in order to get away with some of these things." A summary of congressional responses on the committees considered most useful for campaign fund raising is given below:

Committee	Times mentioned as first, second, or third best for fund raising
Interstate and Foreign Commerce	20
Ways and Means	19
Armed Services	11
Appropriations	10
Banking and Currency	8
Agriculture	5
Post Office and Civil Service	5
Science and Astronautics	5
Merchant Marine and Fisheries	4
Public Works	4
Rules	3
Education and Labor	2
Judiciary	2

Of the two respondents who were members of Interstate and Foreign Commerce (the committee most often cited), one named it the best committee for fund raising and one ranked it third. The member in the sample who was on the Ways and Means Committee ranked it first. Members of both Armed Services and Appropriations (the next two most widely cited committees) said, on the other hand, "I can't really see it" or "I really don't know."

Office Staff and Campaign Staff—An Unenforceable Distinction?

We also asked congressmen to what extent their office staffs became actively involved in raising or disbursing campaign funds. This is a very difficult problem for congressmen. Under Title 18, Sections 602, 603, and 607 of the United States Code, it is a felony for government-paid staff to solicit political contributions, especially in a federally owned or leased facility, which would include the Capitol and a member's field offices. Under the Legislative Appropriations Act, funds are appropriated annually to pay the staff of each member for assisting the legislator in the discharge of "his official and representative duties." The problem is that there has been no explanation of what that means.

A member's office staff is supposed to assist him in his congressional duties in whatever manner he prescribes. Much office time and effort is devoted to servicing the constituency through arranging meetings between constituents and various government officials and following up on "casework" involving such matters as tracing a check that a veteran has not received, arranging for a facilities grant for a municipality, or simply answering the mail. Since a congressman usually serves on only one or two committees, he is generally much more his own legislative assistant than a senator who may sit on three or four committees. But because of the volume of bills introduced and the diversity of constituency interests, staff time is being increasingly devoted to fulfilling the legislative as well as the ombudsman role. In any case, the line between a staff member's congressional duties and his more overt political activity is a very fine and often a very vague one.

Congressional staffs are expected to work at the convenience of the legislators, which may mean they work unusual hours. They have the same rights as other citizens to engage in political activity during their free time. However, since their free time may come during other people's normal working hours, the application of rules governing the political activity of congressional staffs may be extremely difficult. A Washington staff member spending months in his employer's district actively running the campaign may present a fairly clear violation, but it is more difficult to know whether a district office staff member is campaigning on his own time.

The difficulty of regulating the use of staff for political activity became clear during the interviews. Eight respondents admitted that their staffs got involved in fund raising, although a larger number said they scrupulously enforced a clear separation of federally paid staff from campaign activities. Since these activities are against the law, however, these numbers do not necessarily present an accurate picture; some respondents may have thought better of answering the question truthfully. Even so, the number of respondents who admitted violation of the law is quite striking.

The responses to the questionnaire revealed a gap between the standards congressmen have about the use of staff and the way they think their colleagues use staff (table 4-1). The congressmen judged all the activities described on the questionnaire to be unethical but thought that many of their colleagues were involved in some of the activities. They believed, for example, that many committee chairmen would ask professional staff to write partisan speeches for them. They judged a chairman's use of staff to arrange a testimonial luncheon least ethical of the suggested activities and thought that very few congressmen engaged in this practice.

Congressmen use their staffs in many ways that verge on the

Table 4-1. *Mean Scores on Questionnaire Items, Group 1:*
Use of Staff for Partisan Purposes

	Mean score	
Questionnaire item	Judgment of practice[a]	Extent of practice[b]
(44) A committee chairman requests a member of the regular professional staff of his committee to make the arrangements and solicit individual lobbyists to attend a fund-raising testimonial luncheon for the chairman's next campaign.	1.26	2.80
(43) A committee chairman requests a member of the regular professional staff of his committee to go to his constituency and work in his political headquarters during the final month of his election campaign.	1.30	2.83
(16) A legislator instructs his administrative and legislative assistants to put together a $50 per person appreciation luncheon to raise funds for his coming campaign. The staff gets in touch with some lobbyist friends who agree to go on the letterhead of the invitation soliciting attendance, but the staff does all the work in telephoning potential ticket buyers—most of whom have an interest in legislation before the legislator's committee.	1.70	2.55
(7) A committee chairman requests two members of the regular professional staff of his committee to write partisan speeches for him to deliver to various constituent groups.	1.98	2.38

a. Scoring for judgment of practice:
   1 = clearly unethical   3 = probably ethical
   2 = probably unethical   4 = clearly ethical
b. Scoring for extent of practice:
   1 = most congressmen   3 = few
   2 = many   4 = none

partisan. Many respondents admitted that they allowed their staffs to keep lists of constituents who received aid from the congressmen and that the lists were turned over to the fund-raising committee at campaign time. Other members said they avoided doing this because they did not want to change natural, expected, and free congressional service into a quid pro quo.

Some congressmen keep their Washington staffs away from the campaign but allow their district staffs to become deeply involved. One western Democrat did that, but observed, "This bothered me at first, but then I realized that there must be a very good reason why congressional employees were not under the Hatch Act."[1]

Personal staff appear to be widely involved in campaigns. Although much of this activity may be done as "volunteer work" that is "beyond the call of duty," in the words of a north central Republican, Congress has no strong internal norm to limit this activity. Many congressmen see it as perfectly legitimate, despite the present rules.

One of the charges leveled against the late Adam Powell was that he had his wife on the federal payroll at more than $20,000 a year, although she lived neither in Washington nor in his Harlem district but in Puerto Rico, where she admitted that she had virtually no contact with the congressman, much less his constituents. Unfortunately, before they can agree on what constitutes misconduct, congressmen must be presented with a situation this extreme—one that resembles stealing much more than politicking.

The Expenses of Office

Throughout the years congressmen have complained that their salaries and allowances do not permit them to both live

---

1. The Hatch Act (53 Stat. 1147) of 1939 prohibits political activity on the part of most government employees.

comfortably and maintain an adequate office and proper constituent service. Increasingly liberal staff and office allowances and salary boosts that brought congressional pay to $42,500 did not quell the complaints, and a further pay raise was passed in the summer of 1975.

Of all the expenses of office, one of the most worrisome is travel. At the time of our interviews, each congressman could make only twelve government-paid trips annually to his district; the cost of additional travel had to be paid from his own pocket. Since that time, the number of government-paid trips has been increased—first, to forty-two every two years and then, in May 1975, to thirty-two every year.

Even so, many congressmen, particularly in the East, return to their districts every week. Some, including members who live at a considerable distance from the capital, think they must return home as many as eighty to a hundred times a year. These members believe they are compelled to travel to this extent by constituencies that expect such visits either because their representatives' homes are near Washington or because their former representatives conditioned them to expect such appearances. As two congressmen explained during interviews:

—People never think of what the cost is to you. . . . They just regard you as being an hour away. They think nothing of asking you in the middle of the week. When you are as close as I am to your district, the people expect you home all the time.

—The constituency does expect this. And now that jet planes are available, they expect it even more. When you could only get out there by train, you had a good excuse.

A member may feel that frequent visits are required if he is to be reelected, particularly if he is a new congressman or one from a closely contested district. In either case, if he stays in Washington attending to business, he may find himself at a disadvantage when faced by an aggressive challenger operating full time in the district. He knows that unless he regularly returns to his constituency, he too may soon be back there full time. Charges of neglecting the district or abandoning it for Washington can be disastrous.

But some of the responses to the interviews challenged these viewpoints. Discussing pressures from the people back home, a member from the South said: "They don't really expect this. If you go home too much someone will want to know what you're doing home all the time." Another observed: "I think familiarity breeds contempt, and I found that when I quit going home I stopped getting opposition. I think if you're around there too often, why, somebody says, 'Gee, I'm going to run against that guy.'" Describing the dilemma a number of congressmen must struggle with, a western representative lamented, "They get mad when I'm not there, then they get mad when I'm there and might have missed a vote."

Members from the western states, however, found that for the most part their constituents understand that a representative's trips home are costly in both time and money. Constituents in the East, on the other hand, who think of their congressmen as being right next door and able to hop a shuttle airplane home any time, often fail to consider the expense involved in these frequent trips. Nonetheless, easterners make up the bulk of the "Tuesday-to-Thursday Club"—representatives who spend a four-day week in their districts, often for the purpose of maintaining contact with personal business interests, particularly their law firms. Many claim they must maintain such ties to be able to afford to stay in Congress.

Under these circumstances, congressmen see little wrong with the use of unexpended campaign funds for activities that can be considered "service to the constituency." The questionnaire included items on this subject. Respondents judged these items on the "ethical" side of the scale and indicated that they were widely practiced (table 4-2). The most interesting finding is the striking difference between the judgment of these

Table 4-2. *Mean Scores on Questionnaire Items, Group 8:
Use of Campaign Funds for Constituent Service*

	Mean score	
Questionnaire item[a]	Judgment of practice[b]	Extent of practice[c]
(23) Buying flowers to send to the funerals of friends in the constituency.	2.69	2.35
(22) Sending out Christmas cards to several thousand constituents.	2.76	2.12
(25) Entertaining visiting constituents for lunches and dinners when they are in Washington.	2.93	2.12
(19) Books for the legislator's use so he can become better informed on policy matters before Congress.	3.10	1.98
(18) Mail and telephone calls to party groups in the constituency that are not chargeable to the legislator's office allowance.	3.33	1.83
(17) Newsletter.	3.36	1.73

a. All items refer to the following hypothetical situation: A legislator instructs his administrative assistant to manage and raise the funds for his reelection campaign. After the campaign is over, 25 percent of the campaign funds remain unspent. The legislator has his administrative assistant set up a checking account and tells him to use the funds to pay the cost of the items given above.

Respondents were asked to pass judgment on the appropriateness of paying these items from an office expense fund.

b. Scoring for judgment of practice:
    1 = clearly unethical   3 = probably ethical
    2 = probably unethical   4 = clearly ethical

c. Scoring for extent of practice:
    1 = most congressmen   3 = few
    2 = many   4 = none

"service" practices as ethical and the judgment of the personal use of such funds as unethical.[2]

Many of the members interviewed maintained a between-campaign expense fund. In some cases it consisted of unexpended campaign contributions, in others it was raised separately. In the latter instances, the funds were raised through

2. See table 2-2.

testimonial dinners or a "club" whose members contributed a certain amount each year. The club approach appears to be fairly widespread despite the unfavorable attention these funds have received in the past. Usually the club members are local businessmen who receive an "insiders' newsletter," or have dinner privately with the congressman several times a year, or get special attention in other ways.

Between-campaign expense funds spell potential trouble; contributions to an expense fund are not far removed from direct gifts to a congressman, since without the fund he would have to personally pay the costs of his office not covered by his official allowances. Despite the potential for abusing the fund, nearly half of the congressmen interviewed for this study reported some kind of office expense fund. They are not concerned about the practice, especially if the funds are unexpended campaign funds and are used for constituent service. Yet the use of these funds is not necessarily more proper simply because they represent unexpended campaign contributions rather than money collected during a special fund-raising effort. Contributions might simply be collected beyond what is needed for the campaign.

FIVE

The Congressman and His Colleagues

☆ ☆ ☆ ☆ ☆ ☆ ☆ ☆ ☆ ☆ ☆ ☆ ☆ ☆ ☆ ☆ ☆

AFTER EXAMINING the influence of external interests and campaign financing on ethical behavior in the House of Representatives, we gave our attention to internal influences on behavior. Do congressmen have any influence on their colleagues' behavior? One interview question inquired directly about peer group pressure:

Just how much does the average member of Congress concern himself with the conduct of his colleagues? How much does your willingness to accept a colleague's advice on legislative matters depend on his ethical standards?

The majority of the answers showed that congressmen do not oversee their colleagues' behavior. Many of those interviewed expressed some disapproval of the conduct of their colleagues but asked, "What can you do about it?" Almost all were concerned about brazen misconduct because it reflected adversely on the House as a whole. Conduct that is not publicized is tolerated, largely because the congressmen feel impotent to do otherwise. The following responses illustrate the dilemma:

—*We're all human beings, and you just can't be worrying about their conduct. I don't know of any informal sanctions against those who we think violate the ethical codes.*

—*You are not your brother's keeper. He is answerable to the people in his district just as you are. I think whether you listen to him on legislative matters depends on his ability. He might be a bounder on the outside and a wheel on the inside and you would listen to him.*

—I am concerned, but I am isolated. We're all isolated. We have our own offices and we work on individual committees.

—I'm frankly too busy to worry about my colleagues' conduct.

—I would pick the brains of a person even if I ethically didn't agree with him.

—I don't think members care very much about their colleagues' conduct.

—I've got enough trouble and I guess most members feel they have enough trouble and enough work without dabbling in another member's conduct.

—The attitude is not to be too critical. I used to complain to Judge Smith [Howard Smith, former chairman of the Rules Committee], who was a great man, about some of this, and he said there just wasn't much you could do about it.

—It is like your relations with your wife. Your relationship with your constituency is your business. Adam Clayton Powell's sin was that he embarrassed the House. No member really cares if X cleaned up on the sugar bill. But you do care if Congress as such gets a bad name.

Almost no member reported that he would reject advice on legislation from a colleague he considered to have behaved unethically. Nearly all the respondents said they would accept and indeed seek out advice from a member if he were known as an effective legislator, regardless of his ethics. A few noted that they could impose sanctions of a sort—for example, by refusing to assist a particular colleague in matters before their committee—but more said that this was often ineffective and could lead to retaliation.

Reactions to Misbehavior

Most respondents said that there were virtually no formal and few informal penalties for unethical behavior. They might avoid certain colleagues in social situations outside Congress, but this was not presented as a strong control. Responses indicated that unethical behavior is simply ignored in most cases, particularly within the confines of the House, unless it brings the entire House into disrepute. At that time, and only at that time, are sanctions attempted. The congressmen acknowledged that sanctions are primarily motivated by self-preservation.

A particularly apt illustration of this process involved Congressman Sam Steiger of Arizona, who once said on a radio talk show that most members of Congress were not fit to push a wheelbarrow. Many of the congressmen interviewed reported the Steiger case as an example of the kinds of sanctions Congress can impose on its own for improper behavior. After Steiger made his comments, House members gave him the "freeze treatment." They resolutely opposed his bills and denied his requests. A routine land conveyance bill for the city of Glendale, Arizona, came up on the consent calendar[1] soon after his radio appearance. As one member described the situation:

Three members waited on the floor all afternoon for the bill to come up just so they could object. Finally the city fathers of Glendale contacted Congressman Mo Udall to get the bill passed. By that time the message had got through to Steiger's constituents, and that was the purpose of it; their boy could not get anything done in Congress.

Steiger suffered these sanctions not for stealing money, selling his vote, accepting a bribe, or misusing government funds, but for criticizing the other members of the House of Representatives. This, one said, is what "made us all mad."

Congressional interest in self-preservation extends to the in-

1. The consent calendar is a method of dealing quickly with noncontroversial bills by treating them separately from the normal order of legislation. Unanimous consent is necessary for placement of a bill on the consent calendar. One objection will result in carrying the bill over to the next calendar without prejudice. If objected to by three or more members, a bill is immediately stricken from the calendar and cannot be put on again during that session of Congress.

stitutions within Congress. On the questionnaire, we asked the respondents to judge a situation in which a member revealed the confidential positions taken by his colleagues in executive committee sessions. The judgment of this practice fell between "probably unethical" and "clearly unethical," and the members believed that few of their colleagues would reveal confidential proceedings.[2]

When asked what effect the Adam Clayton Powell case had had on their colleagues, most of those interviewed thought that the Powell situation was unique and that therefore it was difficult to generalize about it. An eastern Democrat summarized it this way:

It's hard to know. Powell's problem was that what he did, he did ineptly and flagrantly. Everything he did was being done on a bigger scale, such as the cost of Mendel River's trips in military aircraft, and the use of counterpart funds.[3] I suspect congressmen have been taking broads to Europe since time immemorial. One of Powell's problems was that he took one Negro girl and one white girl.

A border state Republican agreed, saying: "The Powell case was bizarre and not really a measure of the moral climate of Congress. There were racial overtones and backlash overtones. The motives were very hard to determine."

The Powell case did, however, clearly illustrate congressional response to behavior that brings the House into disrepute. The House voted first to exclude Powell from the Eighty-ninth

2. On June 16, 1975, the House Armed Services Committee voted 16–13 to deny access to its files to Democratic Congressman Michael J. Harrington of Massachusetts for having leaked classified information on Central Intelligence Agency operations in Chile. (See *Congressional Quarterly*, June 21, 1975, p. 1286.)

3. Counterpart funds are local currencies that are received from the sale of agricultural products abroad. The U.S. government accepts local rather than hard currencies to give further aid to the recipient nation. The local currencies are then used (under the authorization of the Mutual Security Act of 1954 as amended) for a variety of purposes within that country, including defraying the expense of visiting American dignitaries.

Congress, and when ordered by the Supreme Court to seat him, voted to fine him and strip him of his seniority, including a committee chairmanship. The case also resulted in the establishment of the House "ethics" committee (the Select Committee on Standards of Official Conduct). Other long-term effects of the case were less apparent. Many respondents agreed with the north central Republican who said that "the Dodd and Powell cases had a short-range effect." Another Republican from a border state added:

I think it was a one-shot affair with most of the rank and file, but it did give some impetus and fear of disclosure to some of the members. I worry that if the recommendations of the ethics committee go past this year and members can get elected without having had to approve a code of ethics, it will be awful tough to heat this issue up again.

Several members suggested that "everybody reexamined themselves and their procedures" after Adam Powell and Thomas Dodd got into trouble. The reexamination sometimes took an unanticipated form. One legislator, referring to the Dodd case (in the course of which members of Senator Dodd's staff provided copies of incriminating records from Dodd's files to columnists Drew Pearson and Jack Anderson), observed, "I think everybody is more cautious as to who they hire, and you are less inclined to pick an out-of-state person or to confide in your staff with regard to security matters or confidential matters."

Many of the members interviewed thought that the House ethics committee was not structured to have much of an effect on congressional behavior. A midwestern Republican said:

I think it has been very ineffective. [Name deleted] is on it, and he's not going to be for a rule that would embarrass anybody. Even if he's retiring, he might as well be a lobbyist, and he isn't about to change the way things are.

A western Democrat:

I don't think it has had any effect, and there isn't much movement.

A western Republican:

I have been disappointed. The attitude of the committee seems to be not to make any waves, and this is true of both Democratic and Republican members.

Another western Republican:

Mel Price is a nice guy. I think the fact that he was selected for the chairmanship is significant. He's an easy type. . . . He is not identified with those who are determined to upgrade the image of the House. . . . The fact is that others would have inspired more confidence.

Members from both parties noted that "the leadership appointed all the old war horses" to the committee. A western Republican presented an interesting analysis of the committee's dilemma:

The problem is that every member of Congress is his own operator and is judged by the people whom he represents. I don't think you can set morals, but there are guidelines. I recognize the problem, but I don't think the committee is aggressively pursuing any goal, because they know the people expect more than they can do and the Congress expects less. They don't know which way to turn.

Congress has few sanctions, formal or informal, to control the behavior of its members. What sanctions it has are not likely to be invoked. The members take action only when there is a public outcry or when Congress is embarrassed publicly. As long as unethical behavior does not become public knowledge, it is almost always tolerated. According to one congressman: "The great majority of members are not about to get involved. The attitude is see no evil, hear no evil, speak no evil."

Pressure from Party Leadership or the Executive Branch

When we asked the congressmen in the sample what pressures the floor leadership of their own parties exerted over them, more—both Republicans and Democrats—complained of the lack of party discipline and leadership than the reverse. "The Democratic leadership in the House doesn't exist," one commented. According to another, "the Democratic leadership wouldn't know how to apply pressure." A southern Democrat observed that pressure from leaders "hasn't been any problem. In fact I've seen the opposite. Members have fared awfully well, when they haven't supported the leadership at all and really haven't given them the time of day." Republicans noted that they had heard of heavy pressure being exerted by the Democratic leadership on Democrats, while Democrats suggested the same of the Republican leadership.

The leadership does have some leverage. Committee assignments are one form of leverage, although once a member is on a committee the seniority rules protect him against removal except in the most unusual cases. An eastern Republican noted: "Gerry Ford (then House Republican leader) appoints some to committees who are much less faithful than I am. But I guess they go and see him."

Until recently the rule of seniority was absolute. Once on a committee, a member could stay there and rise in rank and authority until he left Congress. Committee chairmanships automatically went to the most senior member of the majority party on the committee. At the start of the Ninety-third Congress, members of the Democratic caucus agreed that they would vote on whether to continue all committee chairmen. If any chairman lost, the Democratic Committee on Committees would submit another name for vote. Although no chairman came close to being removed at that time, three chairmen were defeated two years later at the start of the Ninety-fourth Congress. In two of the three cases, the positions were filled by the next most senior Democrat on each committee.

Although most of those interviewed in both parties were concerned about the lack of aggressive party leadership, one western Republican complained:

My biggest gripe is about the Republican floor leadership. You're damn right they put unreasonable pressure on an individual. A small group of small men will try to push you into positions that are frankly dangerous for your country. It's not because the vote is right or wrong, but because they feel they can put the Democrats on the spot. This goes on in both parties.

During the interviews, congressmen were asked if the activities of White House or departmental lobbyists posed ethical dilemmas for them. Unexpectedly, they reported few dilemmas, because they experienced little effective executive pressure. The White House or an executive department may request a congressman to act in a certain way or to at least consider a particular position, but there are few ways for those agencies to force compliance.

Although certain congressmen cited isolated examples of payoffs or penalties from the executive branch, most said "they wouldn't dare exert pressure." The comment of a western Democrat about his situation during the Johnson presidency was typical.

No pressure. In fact it's just the opposite. Even though I've caused Lyndon Johnson a number of heartaches, there has never been any intimation that one of my applications for grants for a water or sewer project or housing project would not go through, and I'm very sensitive to something like that.

A Democrat from the Midwest observed of the executive branch: "They will try and persuade you, but when I have balked, I don't recall any recrimination taking place against me, and there have been some real cliffhangers where I have voted against the administration."

Many of the reasons for this lack of effective pressure are rooted in the American political structure. Congressmen are elected from individual districts, commonly through their own personal organizations and without the support or even the coordination of the national party, although state and local parties may be quite important. As long as a member maintains his stature in the district, he can be independent. This independence obviously dilutes presidential or party discipline. A president may withhold warm endorsement, decline to visit the state during a campaign, or seek to withhold benefits from the district as a penalty to a recalcitrant congressman. But these are uncertain sanctions. The congressman may not need a presidential endorsement or visit. Indeed, if he is beyond his first two terms, this is more likely than not. Withholding federal projects from a certain area may not be feasible. Furthermore, the congressman may retaliate by opposing or undercutting the President in other areas. Many congressmen feel that the President needs them more than they need him, and ordinarily they look out for their own political well-being first. The executive agencies (and the President) recognize this.

Many of the congressmen suggested that executive pressure was not nearly as great as the reverse—congressmen pressuring agencies for favorable action. In the interviews, we asked the congressmen how they decided whether and how strongly they would intervene with an agency on constituency matters. We also asked whether they treated regulatory agencies differently from executive departments. Some expressed great hesitancy to intervene with executive agencies. Others, as one put it, "jumped in with both feet." Some members suggested that they carefully screened requests for help with executive agencies and only assisted those with clear merit. Other members freely admitted that they pushed all constituency matters indiscriminately. Two questionnaire items touched on this issue (table 5-1).

The members, from this scanty evidence, seem to judge interference in matters affecting the whole district to be more ethical than interference in ones that affect only one interest in

Table 5-1. *Respondents' Scores on Questionnaire Items about the Practice of Pressuring Executive Agencies for Action*

	Mean score	
Questionnaire item	Judgment of practice[a]	Extent of practice[b]
(39) Relevant appropriations subcommittee chairman insists that executive agency make an undeserved grant to university in his district.	1.67	2.46
(40) Relevant appropriations subcommittee chairman urges a regulatory agency to disallow a common carrier's petition to drop a stop in the chairman's district.	2.49	2.10

a. Scoring for judgment of practice:
   1 = clearly unethical   3 = probably ethical
   2 = probably unethical   4 = clearly ethical
b. Scoring for extent of practice:
   1 = most congressmen   3 = few
   2 = many   4 = none

the district. Responses bore no relation to party affiliation. A southern Republican reported: "I try to follow the same treatment for all cases. Only in severe cases will I call an agency." A midwestern Democrat observed: "I think it's wrong that most members of Congress feel that they should take the part of the constituent on any problem he has. I can't accept that. If I don't feel the cause is right, I just won't do it." A border state Republican said: "I think it's my duty as a member of the House to intervene procedurally but not substantively on behalf of my constituents. We try to get an answer out of the agency, but we don't tell them what the answer ought to be."

An eastern Republican, on the other hand, acknowledged, "I will go 100 percent and then 20 percent more for the constituent, and I assume the constituent is right." A western Republican said, "I'm the only voice that 425,000 people have. Nobody is going to go to bat for them if I don't. I'll write letters and I'll go to the top and I'll demand a fair hearing." A midwestern Republican was even more adamant:

If it's a case problem, I never take no for an answer from the bureaucrats. That's my operational philosophy. I start with the attitude that the constituent is always right, and then I exhaust every avenue since I don't have any confidence in the bureaucratic system. In nine out of ten cases we get good answers to help our constituents as long as we don't relent.

A western Democrat offered an example of a further stage in the process:

If I feel that an agency has made its decision solely to preserve and protect the agency ego, then I get mad. If they don't reverse course when that is involved, then I get vindictive and I will vote against them on a close bill. I instinctively approve of people in Congress who say to the agencies, "If you want my vote, you had better do such and such." The agency interest is too prevailing.

A Republican provided a view of possible congressional retaliation. "The agency doesn't seem to realize that I'm the ranking minority member on the [relevant appropriations] subcommittee, but they'd better bear it in mind in the future."

In their associations with the regulatory commissions, the respondents followed a pattern of caution and deference. Although some claimed to make no distinctions at all between executive departments and the regulatory commissions, the majority were much more reluctant to intervene with the commissions. Congressmen appear to appreciate the judicial nature of the work of the commissions; consequently, they hesitate to interfere. The impropriety of ex parte communications in these cases was mentioned often. Some members will inquire about the status of a matter before the commission, but others will not even do that. Very few claimed not to differentiate at all.

SIX   The View from the House

☆ ☆ ☆ ☆ ☆ ☆ ☆ ☆ ☆ ☆ ☆ ☆ ☆ ☆ ☆ ☆ ☆ ☆ ☆

DESPITE the limitations of this study of standards of behavior in the House of Representatives, its findings should prove useful in determining the need for and the probable success of reform proposals. Responses during interviews and to our questionnaire clearly indicated that congressional behavior may not accord with congressional standards; many practices judged to be of dubious propriety were nonetheless thought to be widely practiced.

Many of the issues treated in the study did not raise ethical questions in the minds of the respondents. The majority regarded behavior in the House as not especially bad, or more precisely, as no worse than that found elsewhere in American society. In general, respondents accepted current practices in Congress and were unwilling to impose further regulations.

Our analysis of five types of conflict of interest—personal financial investments; receiving money, goods, or services from outside sources; assisting private parties dealing with the government; lobbying by ex-congressmen; and deriving personal gain from the use of inside information—demonstrates that congressmen perceive their situation to be unique and much different from that of a member of the executive branch. Consequently congressmen are unwilling to support further regulation of any of the first four items listed. They regard outside financial interests as legitimate and often necessary to supplement congressional income. They see the transfer of money and services to members of Congress as central to current campaign procedures (procedures that continue to result in their

77

reelection). They view assisting private parties dealing with the government as a necessary part of the representative function and consider performing as a lobbyist after leaving Congress to be not only a legitimate occupation but often a form of old-age insurance. They apparently are willing to accept new constraints only in the matter of deriving personal gain from the use of inside information, a practice they deem rare and not all that lucrative.

Vague Standards and Resistance to Change

On the other hand, congressional attitudes and behavior vary widely with respect to specific activities such as campaign fund raising, the maintenance of supplemental office funds, outside business involvements, and the representation of constituents to executive agencies. Standards are vague and sometimes conflicting. Many members find it difficult to reconcile demands on them to promote constituent interests, which are often narrowly conceived, with their own sense of fairness, their own personal needs, and their conceptions of the national interest. Congressmen talk constantly about the dilemmas that arise during their handling of these matters. To the extent that they see certain actions or certain campaign contributions as vital to their political (and hence economic and personal) life, they will behave in ways they may consider improper. Legislators also recognize that each district requires a different political style and prefer to let colleagues cope in their own way with situations that arise.

Other than in fields related to narrowly defined committee responsibilities, congressmen believe that they have the same rights to financial investment that other citizens have. Thus they find it unnecessary to adopt limitations on financial investment for themselves or to seek disqualification from deliberations affecting personal interests, since it would be difficult to define which deliberations would come into question.

The respect that congressmen have for each other's privacy also makes it unlikely that they would require such disqualification. They believe that just as they have the right to financial investment they also have the right to keep those investments private. Congressmen obviously do not like to disclose their finances, and many consider such a requirement discriminatory. They think their financial holdings have little effect on their legislative behavior but recognize the power of public discontent, and many see increased disclosure requirements as inevitable.

A number of lawyer members resist any formal prohibition against the practice of law, but congressmen who have ceased to practice law disapprove of those who have not. Public criticism has increased since 1970 when the New York City bar association published a report expressing disapproval of the practice of law by congressmen.[1] As a result, despite resistance, the number of members practicing law has been shrinking each year and should continue to decline.

While there is no general agreement about the propriety of supplemental office funds, they are widely used. Many congressmen claim their salaries and office allocations are inadequate for them to do their job. Thus, in the absence of large salary and allowance increases, they are not apt to prohibit the use of these funds.

Raising and spending office funds, as well as campaign funds, would cause fewer problems if there were federal election subsidies, restrictions on lobbying expenditures by private interests, increased funding for office expenses, and an independent federal elections agency. Yet resistance to such changes was evidenced in the House action on the campaign finance legislation of 1974. The Senate had passed a sweeping campaign reform bill that included provisions for matching federal subsidies in primary elections and for full federal funding of

1. James C. Kirby, Jr., *Congress and the Public Trust: Report of the Association of the Bar of the City of New York Special Committee on Congressional Ethics* (Atheneum, 1970).

general elections for both the President and members of Congress, plus the creation of an elections commission to enforce the law. The House eliminated the provision for federal funding of congressional elections and significantly reduced the authority of the elections commission. The conference committee report included (at Senate urging) an elections commission to be appointed by the President and congressional leaders and to be approved by a majority of both houses; the commission would have the power to enforce civil but not criminal violations. In turn, public funding of congressional elections was eliminated at House insistence.

The legislation also included ceilings on spending in congressional races and limited contributions from individuals to $1,000 for each primary, runoff, and general election and to an annual total of $25,000. It limited contributions from organizations to $5,000 for each election but did not impose an aggregate limit or restrict an organization's contributions to party-affiliated groups. Honorariums were limited to $1,000 for each item and to a total of $15,000 annually.

The results of our study revealed that, of all the issues analyzed, campaign finance, the receipt of honorariums, and the maintenance of supplemental office funds cause the most severe ethical dilemmas for congressmen. Nevertheless, campaign reform may be the most difficult change to accomplish, since members of the House do not agree on even informal rules of accepted practice. Campaign practices, the amounts spent during campaigns, and the methods of raising such amounts vary widely. Some members restrict the size or the origin of contributions; others have no such limits. Many members employ their staffs in campaigns; others claim not to. The one area of agreement in response to the questionnaire was that the use of campaign funds for personal needs was unquestionably improper, although the members did not agree on a definition of "personal." They generally disavowed some practices, such as the diversion of campaign funds to pay for a spouse's clothes or travel, for home improvement, or for a new car. Other actions that touched on campaigning or constituency service produced much less agreement.

Under the current system, committee and subcommittee chairmen receive the largest rewards in campaign contributions, testimonial dinner receipts, office expense funds, and other benefits. Contributors understandably direct their largesse to those with status and power. Congressmen who receive the largest share are those who have the most power to prevent or facilitate reform and are the least likely to call for increased regulation.

Since it would be difficult to define and enforce a new and more direct distinction between partisan and nonpartisan staff functions, changes in the use of staff cannot be expected. Members who use their staffs in campaigns do not want to give up an arrangement they find useful, and the others are reluctant to interfere with their colleagues' campaign practices.

As long as traditional campaign procedures remain generally unchallenged, members will be extremely reluctant to impose further regulations on their practices. The most obvious reason is the reelection rate of incumbents. The present system works very well for incumbent congressmen, regardless of their complaints about the difficulties of raising funds. They obviously receive adequate funds to be reelected.

Reform: Problems and Prospects

A number of other factors explain congressional restraint or inaction in instituting reform measures. Congressmen have a strong tendency to live and let live, especially in matters of personal and political finance, and they tolerate or even protect a member who may step out of line. They constantly hope no scandal will arise; to help ensure that it will not they say as little as possible about potentially embarrassing matters, accepting them until actual embarrassment occurs. Whenever a member is publicly revealed in an embarrassing, unflattering, or criminal light, the entire Congress suffers, and tolerance comes to an end. In some instances, however, congressmen find themselves discredited because of the actions of others. The Bobby Baker affair and the recent scandals of the Nixon administration demonstrated that even the misdeeds of staff members or of other branches of government may reflect adversely on Congress.

Congressmen see the responsibility for disciplining colleagues guilty of improper behavior as having three dimensions—each congressman personally, the House as an institution, and constituents are all capable of curbing a legislator's actions, although not with equal effectiveness. Often the least effective and most difficult way to discipline congressional behavior is to have individual members attempt it. One member can do little unless he ranks high on a committee in which the errant member is particularly interested. Otherwise, the congressman given the task of discipline is an isolated, powerless unit. Furthermore, the effort to discipline could involve recriminations if the accused member fought back legislatively or personally. A more viable approach is for the House to assume responsibility for defending itself against behavior that weakens it as an institution. It did so by taking formal action against Adam Clayton Powell and informal action against Sam Steiger—but not before one had brought the entire House into disrepute and the other had ridiculed it. This is the vital weakness; unless the House faces public outrage or public ridicule, it is unlikely to take action. Hence the Powell and Steiger cases have not served to deter more private improprieties. That leaves the third approach—having the district take responsibility for the behavior of its chosen representative—which could be the most effective, even if it has not always been in the past. As one member said, "It's up to the district; if they want to send a bum here, what can we do?"

What emerges from these considerations is that the lack of ethical standards in Congress and of any concerted effort to establish strong regulations are rooted in the nation's political institutions. How, then, can the reforms be achieved that low public confidence in government seems to call for? Ironically, the very climate that has accelerated the erosion of public trust may bring forth the answer. The atmosphere surrounding a heavily publicized scandal is conducive to the reordering of old standards; indeed it appears to be vital for such change to take place. The timing of the establishment of the House and Senate ethics committees, of the inclusion of the Code of Official Conduct and limited financial disclosure regulations in the Rules of the House, and persistent proposals for campaign reform all point to this conclusion. Increasing numbers of candidates are finding financial disclosure a political necessity. More of them (or their challengers) are eschewing large campaign donations and attempting to rely on numerous small, open contributions—and are intensively publicizing the effort.

Certainly the passage of significant new campaign finance regulations in the fall of 1974 can be traced to the public outrage engendered by the Watergate scandals. Even so, the House of Representatives strongly resisted the creation of an independent federal elections commission, finally yielded but granted the commission only civil enforcement powers, and refused to agree to public funding of congressional elections. Other areas of concern remain unregulated, but as this study has clearly shown, if the public dissatisfaction that prompted the campaign finance legislation abates, further reform is doubt-' ful. Although for the moment self-interest and political realism in the House are serving to encourage reform measures, the reverse was true in the past. In the absence of continued public pressure, the past may overtake the present again.

Appendix: The Congressman in Context

THE QUESTIONNAIRE was administered to random samples of Washington lobbyists (120 responses), congressional press corps (116), congressional staff (89), and executive department legislative liaison personnel (32). The eight groups of questions, which were the same as those given to congressmen, covered:

1. Use of staff for partisan purposes.
2. Personal use of campaign funds.
3. Favors from private interests.
4. Nepotism.
5. Insertions in the *Congressional Record* favorable to campaign contributors.
6. Promotion of personal interests that coincide with constituent interests.
7. Ties with law firms.
8. Use of campaign funds for constituent service.

The mean scores for all respondents, including the congressmen, are given in table A-1.

The press corps had the worst impression of congressional behavior of any group surveyed. Congressmen had the highest. The next lowest judgment of such behavior was held by the lobbyists and the second highest by the congressional staff. This ranking suggests that the more contact respondents have with congressmen, the more they share the legislators' perceptions.

The press has a more rigid standard for congressmen than do the members themselves for situations affecting personal finances. Newsmen differed significantly with congressmen on groups 3, 6, and 7 (taking favors from private interests, promoting a constituent interest that coincides with one's own financial interests, and maintaining ties with law firms). In each case the press judged the activity to be less ethical than the congressmen did. None of the other groups surveyed differed significantly with the congressmen on these matters, indicating that the newsmen's standards for congressmen not only are higher

Table A-1. *Respondents' Scores on the Questionnaire, by Item Group and Type of Respondent*

Type of respondent	Questionnaire group							
	1	2	3	4	5	6	7	8
	Judgment of practice[a]							
Congressmen	1.55	1.84	1.88	2.29	2.38	2.49	2.50	3.03
Congressional staff	1.81	1.77	1.91	2.31	2.77	2.62	2.50	2.94
Executive department	1.84	1.76	1.70	2.48	2.86	2.46	2.18	3.05
Lobbyists	2.04	2.01	1.79	2.76	3.02	2.56	2.49	2.98
Congressional press corps	1.47	1.89	1.36	2.31	2.49	2.24	2.14	2.91
	Extent of practice[b]							
Congressmen	2.62	2.86	2.58	2.88	2.33	2.09	2.31	2.02
Congressional staff	2.46	2.83	2.41	2.85	2.09	1.98	2.19	2.01
Executive department	2.26	2.73	2.42	2.72	1.65	2.01	2.14	1.78
Lobbyists	2.21	2.66	2.44	2.61	1.78	1.99	2.22	1.89
Congressional press corps	2.09	2.48	2.38	2.49	1.64	1.84	2.05	1.79

a. Scoring for judgment of practice:
  1 = clearly unethical   3 = probably ethical
  2 = probably unethical   4 = clearly ethical
b. Scoring for extent of practice:
  1 = most congressmen   3 = few
  2 = many   4 = none

than those held by the legislators but also are higher than those that other interested and knowledgeable groups set for their representatives. The isolation of the press's responses is probably more interesting for revealing the newsmen's self-image as defenders of the public interest or as hard-nosed realists than for revelations about the other groups.

The findings from the portion of the questionnaire asking how many congressmen the respondents thought would engage in each type of behavior if the opportunity arose again demonstrates striking differences between the congressmen and the press. Responses to all the groups of questions except the one concerning the use of campaign funds for constituent service show that the press thinks that congressmen are much more likely to indulge in the specified behavior than do the congressmen themselves.

Some questionnaire items did not cluster together statistically. Two concerned appropriations subcommittee chairmen putting pressure on executive agencies—by insisting that an undeserved grant be made and by urging the retention of a common carrier stop in the chairman's district. On these two questions, there were no significant differences in the answers of the congressional respondents and the executive agency liaison personnel. The press believed such pressure was much more common than did the congressmen, and the evidence, although scanty, indicates that the press is overly cynical in this regard.

For the questionnaire item (41) dealing with legislators who publicly reveal the confidential positions taken in executive committee sessions, the congressmen's average score was 1.77 (1 = clearly unethical; 2 = probably unethical), while the average for the press corps was 2.36 (3 = probably ethical). Because members of the Washington press corps often depend on the revelation of confidential material for stories, they apparently see a higher motive for engaging in the practice, which they found to be more ethical than did any other group surveyed. No other group of respondents had an average score above 1.89 (congressional staff).

On both the use of staff for partisan purposes and *Congressional Record* insertions (groups 1 and 5), the congressional staff thought such behavior more ethical than the congressmen did. The staffs may approve more highly of their partisan activities than their bosses do either because staff members are unwilling to differentiate between legislative and electoral activities or because they are defensive about their behavior. The difference between staff and congressmen on the issue of placing insertions in the *Congressional Record* that are favorable to campaign contributors seems to show that congressmen see problems with the practice, perhaps because they know that often it is engaged in under obligation or pressure.

The congressional staff sample differed significantly from the congressmen in its judgment of the extent of congressional involvement in specified activities on only one group of questions—that dealing with inserting material favorable to campaign contributors in the *Congressional Record*—which the staff considered a much more common practice than the congressmen did. Presumably the staff is in a position to know about insertions in the *Record*, and it is possible therefore that this practice is more widespread than congressmen admit.

The lobbyists considered the use of staff for partisan purposes, nepotism, and insertions in the *Record* to be more ethical than did the congressmen. It is particularly interesting that the lobbyists found the insertions to be quite proper (mean score = 3.02). Of course, they are often the beneficiaries of this practice. On the other hand, the lobbyists judged taking favors from private interests to be less ethical than did the congressmen, indicating that the lobbyists distinguish between innocent and not so innocent behavior and that they may believe such favors buy influence. The differences in judgment on the nepotism and staff-use questions may indicate that lobbyists are unaware that such activity is against the rules of the House.

The lobbyists thought more congressmen engaged in the use of staff for partisan purposes, nepotism, inserting material favorable to campaign contributors into the *Congressional Record,* and the personal use of campaign funds than did the congressmen themselves. The first three practices were also considered more ethical by the lobbyists, which may explain their expectation of wider congressional indulgence. Although lobbyists considered the personal use of campaign funds to be only slightly more ethical than congressmen did, they nonetheless differed with the congressmen in believing that more legislators use campaign funds in this way. This may reflect cynicism on the part of campaign contributors or the self-protective nature of some of the congressmen's responses.

Question 42 dealt with a member who accepts a $1,000 honorarium for speaking to a group interested in upcoming legislation before the member has decided how he will vote. The congressmen rated it 1.84 (1 = clearly unethical; 2 = probably unethical). The lobbyists, who enjoy the access provided by the distribution of honorariums, considered the practice more legitimate, rating it 2.43 (3 = probably ethical). The lobbyists' score on judging this practice was higher than that of any other group; the congressmen's score was lowest and that of the press was only slightly higher (1.89). Both the lobbyists and the congressional staff felt that congressmen were more likely to accept the honorarium than did the legislators themselves. This finding indicates that this practice may be more common than the congressmen admit. No important differences were found between the congressmen's responses and those of executive agency legislative liaison personnel.

Library of Congress Cataloging in Publication Data:
Beard, Edmund, 1944–
   Congressional ethics.

   1. United States. Congress. House.   2. Political
ethics.   I. Horn, Stephen, 1931–   joint author.
II. Title.
JK1323 .1975.B4   174'.9'328   74-1434
ISBN 0-8157-0855-6

9 8 7 6 5 4 3 2